VACCINE • NOMAD • BARBARIAN
AVOCADO • RESILIENCE •
POMEGRANATE • QUARANTINE
• FUN • C... ...STRUSE•
SEC... ...ICS •
CHO... ...AU •
RO... ...R •
CA... ...Z •
CRIT... ...BIC •
CA... ...NY •
ACRE • CA... ...CURATOF
• GIRL • ADOBE • BERSERK •
AMPHIBOLOGY • BOYCOTT •
AGNOSTIC • TRAMP • NABOB •
CUTE • LACON... • SHAMPOO •
YAHOO ...OSSIL •
CARAVAN • FAX • APOTHEOSIS •

A WORD A DAY

A Daily Dictionary of New and Unusual Words

I0645733

Publications International, Ltd.

Let's get social!

 @Publications_International

 @PublicationsInternational

www.pilbooks.com

Vaccine

A preparation administered by injection, by mouth, or sprayed into the nose, that facilitates the body's immune response, producing immunity to a specific disease.

At the end of the 18th century, an English physician named Edward Jenner became interested in a bit of folklore he had overheard: it was said that milkmaids who came down with the cowpox virus became immune to smallpox. While cowpox might leave the infected with a few local scars, especially on the hands, smallpox was much more deadly. Jenner tested the claim by infecting human subjects with material taken from human cowpox sores. He then exposed his subjects to smallpox—discovering that the process did confer immunity. He published the results in 1798, in a small volume titled *An Inquiry into the Causes and Effects of the Variolae Vaccinae.* His technique soon became humanity's best defense against smallpox.

The Latin term for cowpox, *variolae vaccinae* translates roughly as "cow spots". While Jenner used *vaccinus* ("pertaining to cows") for a specific pathogen, the term was later broadened by other physicians to denote other inoculation procedures.

Nomad

Someone who moves from place to place, often seasonally, and has no fixed residence.

A NEW NUANCE

The modern phrase *digital nomad* traces back at least to a 1997 book of the same name. It refers to those who choose to use technology to move about freely while still being employed.

The word entered English in the mid-16th century, probably as a French loanword. The French word comes from the Latin *Nomas* ("wandering groups in Arabia"), which in turn comes from the Greek *nomas*, a word denoting the activity of roaming from place to place to find pasturage for animals. Even earlier, the word's root *nem* meant something like "allotted land (for pasture)." Though this is speculative, it suggests that the original word from which *nomad* springs came into existence when its speakers stopped being nomads.

Barbarian

Someone from an unfamiliar, foreign place who is considered less civilized or somehow inferior. Also applied generally to people considered cruder than oneself.

Barbarian is an ancient word with a unique origin story. The word comes from the ancient Greek *barbaros*, which was an onomatopoeic coinage: to Greeks of the day, the words that foreigners spoke in their own tongues were characterized as "bar bar bar" (similar to our "blah blah blah")—a kind of babbling nonsense. Initially, then, the primary meaning of the word was "non-Greek babbler." As usage spread, its meaning broadened to "all who are not Greek or Roman."

Historians later used the word to contrast any hostile groups or tribes with the civilizations they attacked. The word bounced from one Romance language to another, eventually entering English in the early 15th century.

Avocado

A fruit (botanically a berry) growing on the *Persea Americana* tree, originating in Mexico. The fruit is edible, oily, and nutty-tasting, with a large, inedible seed. The skin is green- to purple-skinned.

The *avocado* may have evolved thanks to the discerning tastes of extinct megafauna like giant sloths. When humans arrived in central America, sloths were on the way out, but avocados remained. People have been eating avocados in this region for at least 10,000 years. Research indicates they have been cultivated for about 5,000 years.

The word avocado took a curious and twisted route before arriving in the English language. While the first names given to the avocado are unknown, we can pick up the trail around the time the Spanish arrived in the region. They derived the word *ahuakatl* from the local Nahuatl (Aztecan) language. The fact that the word could also refer to a human testicle may or may not have been known to them. In Spanish, the word became *aguacate*. In English, avocados were at first often called avogato pears, later becoming alligator pears. This term existed alongside avocado until recently.

JANUARY 5

Resilience

The ability to maintain strength and health during adversity; showing the ability to recover after something bad happens.

....

Resilience can be found in English at least as far back as the 1640s. The Latin *resilientem* meant "inclined to leap or spring back." It was formed from *re-* ("back") and *salire* ("to leap"). *Salient, consilience, assail,* and *assault* all derive from the same Latin source words.

JANUARY 6

Pomegranate

An orange-sized reddish berry with thick skin, filled with seeds, pulp, and tart juice. The tree has been cultivated since ancient times from the western Mediterranean to the Himalayas and is native to a region covering Iran and northern India.

....

Pomegranate entered English in the 1300s via Old French (*pome grenate*) and Latin (*pomum granatum*). *Pomum* translates to "apple," while *granatum* means "grain." As the "many-seeded apple," the pomegranate frequently represented fertility in ancient cultures.

FRUITY FACT

....

Pomona was the Roman goddess of fruitful abundance and fruit trees in particular.

JANUARY 7

Quarantine

A situation or period of time in which someone or something is kept in isolation in order to prevent the spread of a disease.

While the concept behind the word *quarantine* traces back to antiquity, the word itself comes to us from the time of the Black Death, the plague which swept across Europe in the 1300s and wiped out a third of the population. In the Venetian dialect of the Italian language, *quarantena* meant "forty days." The word was used to refer to the period during which incoming ships had to stay offshore before disembarking. This holding period was implemented to help halt the spread of the plague.

Similar versions of the word also entered English via Latin and French and once had several other definitions. In the early 16th century, the period of 40 days referred to the time in which a widow had a right to remain on her deceased husband's property. As *quarentyne*, it referred to the desert where Christ fasted for 40 days.

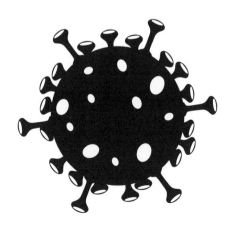

Fun

Something or someone that provides amusement or enjoyment.

Sometimes the simplest words contain the trickiest etymologies. *Fun* is a case in point. The word may have entered the language before the 1600s, but records are unclear. Its original meaning was primarily negative. Fun may come from the Middle English *fonne*, which meant "a fool or stupid person." As a verb, this word meant "to cheat or trick." Even in the 18th century, Samuel Johnson dismissed fun as a "low cant word." By the early 19th century, fun referred to jokes and general clowning behavior. By the end of the century, usage had become more benign—fun could be any kind of pleasurable experience.

Chindōgu

A weird tool, often created with humorous intent, that has little or no use in the real world.

Of Japanese origin, this word entered the English language in the mid 1990s. The term was coined by Kenji Kawakami, an editor of a home shopping magazine. He used the term to describe bizarre consumer inventions that were "un-useless." The concept caught on, and soon the art of inventing *chindōgu* became a worldwide phenomenon. Examples of chindōgu include the toilet paper hat, glow-in-the-dark camouflage, and an electric fork to gather up spaghetti.

JANUARY 10

Abstruse

Something hard to comprehend.

The Latin source word *abstrusus* means "concealed, secret." Specialized words like *abstruse* often pass in and out of common usage, but in this case the word has managed to stay in rotation since the 16th century. Though never a common word, it has maintained usage particularly in literary instances. Thank you, Milton, Swift, and English professors everywhere.

JANUARY 11

Cinnabar

Red mercuric sulfide, often used as a pigment. Used to describe a deep and vivid red.

Cinnabar is probably most familiar to us as a ruddy hue on a color palette. It originally came into use in English in the 15th century to describe mercury ore. The Old French *cinabre* came from Latin *cinnabaris*, which in turn came from the Greek *kinnabari*. Possibly the Greek word came from a Persian word. In these earlier languages, it kept its primary meaning in relation to a mercury ore. For at least ten thousand years, cultures around the world have mined cinnabar to extract the precious pigment. Cinnabar has been found in ancient Egyptian tombs and on the skulls and bones of Neolithic cultures, from Spain to China.

Biometrics

The measurement and analysis of human characteristics (body shape, fingerprints, palm veins, voice patterns, DNA, gait, odor/scent, and behavioral, among others) as a means of personal identification.

The controversial field of *biometrics* is a growing part of modern society. On the governmental side, the Office of Biometric Identity Management contains a massive biometric repository (more than 260 million unique identities) for the Department of Homeland Security's use. On the commercial side, more and more consumer devices are being embedded with tools like fingerprint and voice recognition. A major concern regards privacy—consumers want to know what happens to the unique data they're providing and whether it will find its way to third parties.

There are positive tradeoffs to automated identity recognition. in law enforcement, criminals can be more easily tracked and found. Consumer products may offer more convenience and security. In an age of identity theft, the higher security offered by biometrics is very attractive. Privacy invasion or security enhancement?

Chocolate

A food made from processed cacao beans, typically made into a candy or confection, or added to desserts or beverages.

....

The Mexican Spanish word *chocolate* entered English in the early 17th century. The word's origins seem to be from Nahuatl, but possible cross-contamination from similar-sounding words makes the etymology murky. One story involves the 1519 expedition to Mexico led by Cortez. When his party arrived in the Aztec capital city, they were offered a beverage called *tchocoatl*. This word roughly translates as "bitter water." However, another story identifies *chicolatl* ("beaten drink") as the source. This word probably derives from the word *chicoli* (frothing stick). Both derivations make sense but neither is proven. Another theory has the Spanish modifying a source word to make it sound less like the vulgar Spanish word for excrement.

Chocolate itself comes from the seeds of the cacao tree. The journey from seed to chocolate is fairly complex: the seeds must be harvested, separated from pods and pulp, fermented, dried, and roasted. The hull is then removed, and the nibs undergo further processing. The resulting cocoa butter, cocoa liquor, or cocoa powder can then be combined with other ingredients like milk and sugar to create chocolate.

Portmanteau

A large suitcase; a made-up word formed by blending two or more distinct words into a new one.

....

The word *portmanteau* is an example of itself. The word comes from two French words that have been blended together to create its first meaning: *porter* ("to carry") and *manteau* ("mantle"). Lewis Carroll created its second meaning in 1871 in his novel, *Through the Looking Glass.* In the story, Humpty Dumpty explains the strange words in the poem "Jabberwocky."

Well, "slithy" means "lithe and slimy." "Lithe" is the same as "active." You see it's like a portmanteau—there are two meanings packed up into one word.

Carroll's definition caught on, as did a number of his own portmanteaus, like *chortle* (chuckle + snort).

Examples of modern portmanteaus include *pixel* (pix + element), *cosplay* (costume + play), *blog* (web + log), and *gastropub* (gastronomy + pub). Older portmanteaus include *electrocute* (electro + execute), *brunch* (breakfast + lunch), *dramedy* (drama + comedy), *spork* (spoon + fork), *motel* (motor + hotel), and *sitcom* (situation + comedy).

Robot

A machine resembling a living creature that can move independently and perform physical tasks or complex actions.

Czech writer Karel Capek introduced the word *robot* (coined by his brother) while writing the 1920 play *R.U.R.* ("Rossum's Universal Robots"). The play was translated into English in 1922, and the word found its way into common usage. The play described a fictional company that made human-looking machines (creations we would term *androids* today). The machines were created to perform hard tasks and drudgery. The play is hardly optimistic, and the story describes a bloody revolt that ends with a robot victory.

The word comes from the Czech *robota*, which means something like "compulsory service." It traces back to *robotit* ("to work, drudge") and is related to Old Church Slavonic *rabota* ("servitude") and *rabu* ("slave").

Robots quickly became a staple of science fiction. Science fiction writer Isaac Asimov later coined *robotics* to describe this field of study.

Neologism

A new word or expression.

Like *portmanteau*, *neologism* is an example of itself. The word comes from the French *néologisme*, and entered English in the 18th century. The word's roots trace back to the Greek *neo* ("new") and *logos* ("word"). Neologisms are frequently formed by combining existing words (as with portmanteaus). They are typically recent terms or phrases, often in the process of entering common use, but not always fully accepted into mainstream usage.

Cider

Raw juice derived from fruit (usually apples), that has not been filtered to remove sediment; often made sparkling via fermentation or carbonation.

Depending on what part of the English-speaking world one is from, *cider* may be alcoholic or not. U.S. usage tends to go with the latter. The Middle English *sider* is a borrowing from an Anglo-French word that ultimately traces back to the Latin *sicera*. This word in turn traces back to the Hebrew *shekhar*, a word that meant "strong drink."

Cider, both hard and otherwise, was once a staple beverage in colonial America. Homesteads frequently had apple orchards. Local water was not always safe to drink, so plentiful cider became the national beverage, especially in rural areas.

Cannabis

A tall herb with tough fibers native to parts of Asia. Used for its psychoactive and medicinal effects. As hemp, a fiber with industrial applications.

Demonized by some, revered by others, *cannabis sativa*'s recent legalization in many U.S. states has kept the debates over its relative benefits and drawbacks in the spotlight. Regardless of current controversy, cannabis has a recorded history of usage that goes back three thousand years. Archeological finds suggest that human usage for psychoactive purposes goes even further back; physical evidence has been found from the Middle East to China, in the form of seeds, resin, and chemical residues.

The English word is derived from the Greek *kannabis*. The Greeks borrowed the word, probably from a neighboring language like Scythian or Thracian. That borrowing also made its way into Proto-Germanic, becoming *hanapiz*. This word evolved into *hanap* and entered Old English, eventually becoming *hemp*. The Anglo-French *canevaz* (which became *canvas* in modern English) also comes from this same ancient source word.

Glitz

Extravagant in appearance; showy or flashy.

Glitz is a back formation from the adjective *glitzy*, a relatively young word in English that has Yiddish and German roots and came into common usage at some time in the 1950s. The Yiddish term also implied "bad taste," but this meaning is not always evident in contemporary usage. The German source word *glitzern* means "sparkle." The related English word *glitter* has been in circulation since the Middle Ages. All of these words can be traced back to the Proto-Indo-European *ghel*, a word which gave us *gold*. So anyone that tells you "all that glitters is not gold" doesn't know their etymology.

Spritz

To spray or disperse something, typically a liquid.

Spritz entered English from a Yiddish or German source (*spritzen*, "to squirt") in the late 19th century, maintaining its essential meaning. We derive the beverage name *spritzer* from this word. Its root comes from the Proto-Germanic *sprut*, and gave us the modern English *sprout*.

Critic

A professional evaluator of a specific subject; anyone who articulates an opinion on a subject, specifically about its value, truth, relative merit, or technique.

Critics have probably been around forever, but the word itself shows up in English in the 1580s as *critick*. Semantically, the word has always carried the negative overtones of faultfinding and censure. Its source words are the French *critique* and the Latin *criticus* ("judge, censor"). The Latin word comes from the Greek *kritikos* ("to pass judgement") and is based on an older Proto-Indo-European root word (*krei*) meaning "to sieve or distinguish." It seems the art of judging the works of other people has been around for a very long time.

Interestingly, *krei* has a particularly robust family tree. It is the root of many other words having to do with discernment and judgement, including: *certain, crime, crisis, criterion, decree, discern, disconcert, discreet, discriminate, excrete, garble, hypocrisy, recriminate, riddle,* and *secret*.

Mortgage

A conditional loan for the purchase of property, secured by a lien on the property, that becomes void upon full payback.

....

The Old French word *morgage* entered English in the 14th century. It evolved from *mort gaige* ("dead pledge"), so called because the agreement "dies" when the loan or debt is paid or payment ceases.

The concept of the *mortgage* appears in English common law documents as far back as 1190. The idea introduced in these documents detailed creditor protection: a mortgage was a conditional sale, with the creditor holding title to the mortgaged property. Mortgages came to America with the English. They weren't as friendly to borrowers at first. Home buyers typically had to pay 50% up front and pay off the difference over a few years. This excluded poorer classes of people from purchasing their own homes. Even for those able to scrape together the down payment, there was a higher likelihood of defaulting.

One of the results of the Great Depression was the creation of the Federal Housing Administration (FHA) in 1934. Policies introduced by the FHA created safeguards for lenders and eased conditions for buyers. The creation of the 30-year mortgage, with its reduced down payment, for example, allowed more Americans to buy homes.

JANUARY 23

Acerbic

Biting, sharp, critical, or sarcastic in words or tone.

....

The first, primary meaning of the word had to do with taste—anything sour, harsh, or bitter might be described as acerbic. It was coined in the 19th century by adding *-ic* to the adjective *acerb*, a rarely-used word that has been around since the 17th century. For most of that time it was used to describe sour-tasting foods. The Latin source word, *acerbus*, also meant "harsh." This source word also provides us with *exacerbate*.

JANUARY 24

Cannibal

One that eats the flesh of its own species.

....

Christopher Columbus is indirectly responsible for this word's presence in English dictionaries. The Spanish word *canibal* or *caribal* is a garbling of the name for a group that lived in the Lesser Antilles. Columbus described his encounter with them after his first voyage. Subsequent controversial legends told of their practice of eating human flesh. Since people have always been quick to accuse other cultures of cannibalism, it would be surprising that English had to wait until the 16th century for such a purposeful word. In fact, there was at least one earlier word that addressed the concept: the Old English *selfæta* (literally "self-eater").

Geek

Someone who is an expert or enthusiast, especially in a technological field, formerly used pejoratively.

The meaning of *geek* has undergone repeated semantic drift since it began circulating in American carnival slang at the beginning of the 20th century. It may have come from the same root as *geck*, a word also found in German and Scandinavian languages. Older meanings in these languages included "to mock or cheat" and "to croak." Its first known English usage was in the 1870s. By the mid-20th century, it was firmly associated with circus sideshow acts, particularly with performers who bit off animal heads or performed similar acts.

The association with technology was in place by the 1980s and was especially used by teenagers as a pejorative term for socially inept computer enthusiasts. Because of that association, usage exploded in the 1990s as consumer computer usage grew. The word began losing its purely negative connotation along the way. While the word can still be an insult, depending on the context, it typically now connotes excitement and enthusiasm (to "geek out") on the part of someone who is knowledgeable or a specialist in some subject.

Irony

A usually humorous scenario in which words are used to express something other than their literal meaning; a situational incongruity between intent and result.

Critics have noted that the meaning of *irony* in contemporary usage varies wildly according to user and context. The word may now be used in contexts where sarcasm, parody, satire, mockery, or coincidence would be the better choice. It entered the English language in the 16th century. Its Latin source word *ironia* comes from the Greek *eironeia*, and meant something like "feigned ignorance." This stance of dissimulation was particularly connected with the affected ignorance used in Socratic dialogues to expose ignorance.

The word may continue to broaden and change, but meanwhile, here's a clear and agreed upon example of situational irony from a 1905 O. Henry story. In "The Gift of the Magi," Christmas presents are exchanged by a young couple. Della sells her beautiful hair to buy a pocket watch fob for Jim. Jim sells his pocket watch to buy ornamental combs for Della. These actions destroy the value of the gifts they exchange: an irony.

Acre

A parcel of land equaling 43,560 feet (4,047 meters), commonly used as a measuring unit in the U.S. and England.

....

While urban populations may not have a keen grasp of the size of an *acre*, this unit of measurement has been important in real estate and agriculture since medieval times. The Old English *æcer* (related to the Germanic *akraz*) meant "open land" or "tilled field." It seemed to have a prior sense of "untenanted" or "untilled" prior to this, but changed with the advance of agriculture. As a unit of measurement in Old English, it came to mean the amount of land a yoke of oxen could plow in a single day.

Cantaloupe

A commonly cultivated muskmelon with a thick, hard rind and orange flesh.

....

Cantalupo was a papal summer residence located in the Sabine Hills outside Rome. The estate imported the melon and began growing it in the early 18th century. The usual story is that the melon took its name from this location. However, it's worth noting that there are seven towns in Italy called Cantalupo and one in France called Cantaloup. Multiple varieties of melons had already been cultivated in Mediterranean countries for centuries. At any rate, the *Gardeners Dictionary* was published in 1739, and that is our first source for the word in English.

Curator

One who cares for or superintends something.

The Latin source word, *curator* (from *curatus*), meant "overseer, guardian." Early English definitions, beginning in the 14th century, tied this word to ecclesiastical functions, and subsequently, to superintending offices within institutions like libraries, galleries, and museums.

The word remained stable semantically for a long time, and was associated with learned professionals engaged in typically highbrow cultural activities. But in the recent past, there has been a broadening and democratizing of its usage, leading to some accusations of self-aggrandizement (does creating an iTunes playlist, cheese board, or experience really make one a curator?) Regardless of how we or disgruntled museum staff may feel about it, the change in meaning has gone mainstream. Even cocktails can have curators. The word may now simply refer to anyone who has carefully and thoughtfully organized a specific subject, be it art, music, food or drink, clothing, personal grooming, or digital content.

Girl

A female human child.

....

Girl is a common English word with a surprising backstory. Its origins are obscure, going back to the 13th century, but apparently not common before then. Some scholars consider it a derivation of the Old English *gierela* ("garment"). In former times, the Latin *garrulus* ("chattering, talkative") was considered probable, but this origin has been discarded. Others see a connection with the conjectural *gyrele*, a word from Proto-Germanic. Initially, *gyrle* (or *gurle*, among other spellings) could refer to any young person, and could mean male or female children. Earlier definitions might have been broad enough to include any immature animal. Restriction of the word to females only happened in the 1400s. By about 1530, the word implied "any young unmarried woman."

Adobe

Building material made of straw and sun-dried earth.

....

Adobe is a borrowing from the same Spanish word. It entered American English in the 18th century. As a building material, it has been used for thousands of years and can be found in many parts of the world. Possibly the word may trace all the way back to the Coptic *tube* and be represented in Egyptian hieroglyphics.

Berserk

Frenzied or crazed behavior.

Today, to be or to go *berserk* is to be frenzied out of one's mind, with a connotation of violent behavior. That violent connotation was once the word's primary meaning. The word comes from the Icelandic *berserkr*, a word for a powerful Norse warrior who displayed a wild and uncontrolled fury on the battlefield. In other words, a typical Viking warrior. (Or at least this is the popular image of what a typical Viking was like. In reality, the typical Viking was more likely to be a peaceful merchant than the ransacking and pillaging barbarian of lore. But, evidently, there were enough of the ransacking and pillaging types among the Scandinavian nations to give them all a bad name.) The ultimate origin of the Icelandic word is somewhat uncertain, but it probably comes from *bear + sark*, a type of shirt or tunic. So a berserk or berserker was literally a bearskin-clad warrior.

The word made its English appearance as early as 1814 in the original Icelandic sense of "a fierce warrior." By the middle of the 19th century, however, the word was being used as an adjective in English, meaning "violent or frenzied."

Amphibology

An ambiguous sentence or phrase that can be understood in multiple ways.

Here's a classic from Groucho Marx: "One morning I shot an elephant in my pajamas. How he got into my pajamas I'll never know." It's one of Marx's most famous jokes—but what makes it so funny?

He's using *amphibology*: a grammatically ambiguous statement that appears to mean one thing at first but, upon rereading, could mean another—a bit like the verbal equivalent of an optical illusion. In the first sentence, the prepositional phrase "in my pajamas" could refer to the speaker or to the elephant—although of course no one automatically thinks this upon hearing it. So when the pajamas are unexpectedly assigned to the elephant, the laugh line turns the listener's expectations upside down.

Amphibology comes from the Greek word *amphibolos*, meaning "doubtful, ambiguous," which in turn comes from the prefix *amphi-*, meaning "on both sides," and from *ballein*, meaning "to throw." So an amphibolous statement is one with the ability "to throw on both sides"—or, in more modern terms, "to swing both ways" (grammatically).

FEBRUARY 3

Boycott

To protest by refusing to buy, use, or participate in something.

....

Boycott is an eponym, or a word that comes from a person's name. In this case, the namesake is Captain Charles Boycott, the agent of an absentee landlord in Ireland. In 1880, Boycott evicted tenants who were demanding reduced rents. In response, the Irish Land League organized an effort to ostracize Boycott. He was unable to hire workers, buy goods, or receive mail. With help, Boycott managed to get the autumn crop harvested, but it cost him more than the crop was worth. At the end of 1880, Boycott resigned his post and returned to England, the action against him having worked beyond the wildest imaginings of its organizers. The eponym caught on immediately.

FEBRUARY 4

Agnostic

Someone who is not committed to a belief in either the existence or nonexistence of God.

....

Agnostic was coined by T.H. Huxley, reputedly in 1869. His source was the Greek *agnostos* ("unknown, unknowable"). The word's meaning is sometimes confused with that of *atheist*, but the two words have distinct meanings. An atheist does not believe in the existence of any gods, whereas an agnostic doesn't know whether there is a god or gods or whether it is even possible to prove the matter one way or the other.

Tramp

A loud or heavy tread; someone who travels by foot and typically has no fixed abode.

. . . .

Tramp in the sense of "walk heavily" entered English in the 14th century. It has a Germanic root, *trampen*, meaning "to stamp." As a noun meaning "vagabond or vagrant," it dates to the 17th century. The latter usage blossomed in 19th century England and America, thanks to the consequences of the Industrial Revolution as migrant labor increased and housing shortages occurred.

FEBRUARY 6

Nabob

Historically, a ruler of India's Mughal empire; someone affluent or of significant prominence.

. . . .

The Mughal Empire once sprawled across most of India, existing from the early 16th century until its dissolution by the British Raj in 1857. It was a powerful and wealthy empire, and its elites were too. The Urdu word *nawab* denoted a powerful ruler of the empire. The word passed into English colloquial use and gradually grew to include Europeans who had made their fortune in India, usually via the East India Company. Prevailing attitudes about this practice weren't exactly positive, so usage was often sarcastic. That sense has mostly disappeared.

Cute

Having an attractive and often youthful appearance.

It may seem that we are living in an era of cataclysmic cuteness. Evidence of our obsession with all things fuzzy and cuddly can be found in innumerable websites, movies, products, and phenomena. Pictures of kitties, puppies, babies, and cupcakes abound. Human love for all things *cute* may be hardwired into our natures, but the word itself hasn't always meant the same thing. Cute is actually the child (the puppy, if you will) of *acute*. It comes to us through the process of *aphesis*, or the loss of an initial (typically unstressed) vowel, and it originally meant the same thing as its progenitor—"clever, keen-witted, sharp, shrewd." A century or so after its appearance, cute had become a substitute for *cunning*—a word whose evolution has followed a similar trajectory—in the sense of "quaintly interesting or pretty, attractive." While this variation gets us closer to today's connotations of cute, it doesn't quite apply to our puppy-and-kitten-coddling culture. In fact, the *Oxford English Dictionary* entry on cute, which lists the contemporary colloquial sense as "attractive, pretty, charming," might need an update, since this definition seems a little too cunning and not nearly cutesy enough.

Laconic

Using a minimum amount of words; sparse in conversation.

....

Laconia was an ancient Greek region in the orbit of the infamously austere Sparta. Its people had a reputation for brevity and dry wit. *Laconic* comes directly from this place name. A famous example of laconic wit comes from the time when Philip II of Macedon's army invaded the region. He reputedly sent a message stating "If I attack you, I will burn your crops and enslave your people." Sparta answered with one word: "If."

Shampoo

A preparation used to wash and clean hair.

....

Depending on what part of the world you lived in, asking for a shampoo before the middle of the 19th century could have resulted in either a nice massage or a confused stare. The Anglo-Indian word *shampoo* first appeared in 1762, and denoted a kind of body massage. Its derivative Hindi word *champo* meant "to press and knead the muscles." New bathing and grooming practices from India made their way back to England, and the word eventually became restricted to the practice of washing hair or the preparation itself.

FEBRUARY 10

Yahoo

A yokel, lout, or boorish person.

Jonathan Swift's *Gulliver's Travels* was published in 1726. He coined the word *yahoo* to describe a group of filthy, stinky, human-like creatures with repulsive habits. "I never beheld in all my travels so disagreeable an animal," the narrator noted. Unfortunately, the speaker seemed to share many similarities to the yahoos, at least in appearance. Swift invented the creatures to point out some of the uglier qualities and habits of contemporary Europeans. The word immediately caught on. It came to be used for any person deemed stupid or repulsive in some way and was particularly popular in the 18th century.

AS A BACKRONYM

The name of the American web services provider Yahoo! is an example of a *backronym*—an acronym that coincides with an existing word. In this case, the backronym stands for "Yet Another Hierarchical Officious Oracle." It was coined around 1995.

As an expostulation, the word has been exuberantly flying out of English-speaking mouths for a less certain amount of time, as have other onomatopoeic words like *woo-hoo, yeehaw*, and *yippee*.

Apotheosis

A perfect example of something; the best part; elevation to a transcendent position.

Apotheosis was part of the wave of highbrow Latin word borrowings that flooded English in the 16th and 17th centuries. It originally referred quite literally to deification (specifically, the process by which important or royal personages were elevated to a state of godhood), as, for example, when a Roman emperor was declared a god after his death. This is revealed in the word's two roots: *apo* here means "change," and *theos* means "god."

From its initial sense of "elevation to divine status," the word's meaning came to include putting someone on a very high pedestal due to their abilities, virtues, or powers. In contemporary usage, an apotheosis might imply "the ultimate example of the best of something."

The root *apo* comes from a Proto-Indo-European word meaning "off, away." It's a rich source for the English language, and can be found in many words, including the following: *after, aperitif, aperture, apocalypse, apology, apostle, apostrophe, apothecary, awkward, ebb, eftsoons, off,* and *offal.*

Polite

Socially correct or polished; having courtesy, consideration, and tact.

The word *polite* provides a good example of the process of semantic broadening. The adjective first appeared as a direct Latin borrowing in the late 14th century. Its first meaning in English was a literal one—"smooth, polished." As had happened in Latin, by 1500 the word was being used to mean "refined, cultured," a sense that survives today chiefly in the phrase *polite society*. Finally, the sense of "courteous, well-mannered" developed some time in the mid-18th century.

We derive the word from the Latin verb *polio*, meaning "to smooth, to polish." Its past participle, *politus*, and adverbial form, *polite*, came in that language to mean "cultured, refined"—a metaphorical polish. We see the same development of meanings in French, where the word *poli* appears around the year 1160 with the meaning of "smooth, shiny." Later, the word's meaning was broadened and applied to words and diction with a meaning of "careful, well-chosen." A similar pattern occurred at about the same time in Spanish and Italian.

Conurbation

An extended and continuous metropolitan area made up of various urban communities including outlying suburbs and towns, the result of urban sprawl.

Scottish biologist and urban planner Patrick Geddes coined this word in his 1915 book *Cities in Evolution.* In it, he noted that the new technologies of electric power and motorized transport were allowing cities to spread and join together. He thought a name was needed for these thickly populated areas that had fused together into something new—something more apt than "even bigger city." Geddes took *urbs* (Latin for "city") and joined the Latin prefix *con-* ("together") and the English suffix *-ation* to it.

FEBRUARY 18

Hypocrisy

Behavior that does not correlate with what someone claims to believe is right; feigning to be something one is not.

First appearing in Middle English as *ypocrisye*, this word comes to us via typical borrowing channels. The Anglo-French word came from the Latin *hypocrisis*, which in turn was borrowed from the Greek *hypókrisis* ("acting on stage, pretending to be something other than what one is"). That's already a lot of meaning to pack into one word. The modern meaning provides us with the perfect semantic rock to fling at all the lying, conniving, boasting, and spinning that comes our way.

Cult

A group (often religiously-oriented) that has set itself apart from general society in some way and that has beliefs or practices that many consider extreme.

....

Cult, in modern usage, is a word loaded with negative connotations. A cult is typically set apart from the general population and its membership tends to be small. Or, to paraphrase Frank Zappa's cynical take, it's a religion without any real estate. Along with *culture* and *cultivate*, it comes from the Latin *cultus*. Early definitions from the 17th century were associated with religious worship. By the 19th century, the word was gaining a pejorative sense and was specifically used in connection with the fraudulent or spurious in religion.

Alias

Indicating an additional or assumed name; otherwise known as.

....

Coming straight from Latin, *alias* originally meant "in another way," or "at another time." Embedded in the word is *al*, another hardworking Proto-Indo-European root that has given English *alibi, alien, allergy, alter, altruism, eldritch, else, other, outrage, outre, parallel, ulterior,* and *ultimate,* among others.

Digital

Relating to electronics devices; relating to data composed of binary digits; relating to fingers and toes.

Digital has many meanings, depending on context. It's a splendidly flexible word—just like human fingers. In its most common contemporary usage, the word refers to digital media, digital devices, or modern computing in general. This usage coincides with the rise of such technology, of course, but prior to the computer age, the word's primary meanings referred to numbers or fingers and toes. From the 17th to the 20th century, that meaning remained unchanged, and the word was not common. The Latin source word *digitalis* (from *digitus*) meant "finger or toe." This is also where we derive the English *digit* from. The numerical sense grew from the practice of counting numerals under ten on our fingers.

In the past decade, a looser meaning has emerged. We now use terms like *digital economy* and *digital art* and extend it to the virtual counterparts of real-world objects (*digital shopping cart*, *digital ink*). This broadening may signify an eventual decline in usage in coming decades: once something is solely digital, there will no longer be a need to specify it as such.

Pensive

Sadly thoughtful or dreamy.

....

The French word *pensif* meant "thoughtful," and *penser* meant "to think." *Pensive* entered English in the 14th century with that meaning. By the next century, its sense had been overlaid with an emotional tone of melancholy. To think intensely about something and be worried about it as well is to be pensive.

FEBRUARY 23

Hockey

A team sport played on a smooth ice surface, whose object is to move a puck into the opposing team's goal with a hockey stick.

....

This may come as a surprise, but the sport of *hockey* is far older than the sports of football, baseball, or basketball. In fact, the game has roots going back thousands of years.

The countries of Canada, England, and Scotland are usually credited with giving the game its modern shape. The word's origins are obscure. One common conjecture is that the word is related to the old French *hoquet* ("shepherd's staff"). The word may also have Gaelic roots.

GAME PIECE

....

The origin of *puck* is also mysterious. Two reasonable derivations are from the English verb *poke*, and the Irish *poc*, a word associated with the game of hurling.

Mondegreen

A word or phrase that is misheard, especially in song.

A classic example of a *mondegreen* is the Jimi Hendrix lyric, "'Scuse me while I kiss the sky," which many have mistakenly heard as "Scuse me while I kiss this guy." The word was coined by writer Sylvia Wright in 1954, inspired by her own mishearing of a line in the old Scottish ballad "The Bonnie Earl o' Moray." The line goes, "They have slain the Earl o' Moray and laid him on the green," but she thought it went, "They have slain the Earl o' Moray and Lady Mondegreen." She wrote an article about her "enlightenment" in *Harper's* in 1954, which popularized the term.

Other mondegreens include animals ("Olive, the other reindeer" who used to call Rudolph names, apparently), directions (Creedence Clearwater Revival's observation that "there's a bathroom on the right" instead of a bad moon on the rise), and the mysterious figure Richard Stans (made famous by the United States Pledge of Allegiance, which doesn't quite go, "and to the republic, for Richard Stans"). Maybe he's the one who's responsible for making the nation "invisible."

FEBRUARY 25

Dude

Informal term of address for men and boys; guy, fellow.

There has been some contentious theorizing over the etymology of *dude*, but one thing can be agreed on: it began as a slang term and came into usage in the United States in the 1880s. It could have come from a German word meaning "fool." Or it could have been a shortening of Yankee Doodle. The term eventually came to mean a city slicker vacationing in the Wild West. It has since evolved into a general term for a guy, or in some cases, it's an affectionate word for a member of one's own group. Basically, "dude" has come full circle from outsider to insider.

FEBRUARY 26

Supercilious

Acting haughty or patronizing.

This word applies to those people who think they are better than their peers and show an overtly cool or aloof disdain. Interestingly, the word's origin perfectly describes the actions of these very people, with chins raised and eyebrows lifted. The Latin word *supercilium* can be broken down into two words that mean "eyebrow" (*cilium*) and "above, proud" (*super*).

Kaleidoscope

A segmented tube with a viewing hole through which one can see a colorful pattern. Patterns can be manually shifted into new configurations.

A *kaleidoscope* contains loose, sliding bits of colorful material held between two plates. Mirrors within the tube are placed so that a symmetrical image always appears to the viewer. Turning the end changes the image.

The literal meaning of this word is "observer of beautiful forms." It was coined in 1817 by its inventor, Sir David Brewster (1781–1868), from the Greek *kalos* ("beautiful"), *eidos* ("shape"), and *scopos* ("watch" used as a suffix on the model of "telescope"). The figurative meaning of a "constantly changing pattern," is attributed to poet George Gordon, Lord Byron (1788–1824), who received one as a gift from his publisher.

Although the instrument is now considered a child's toy, Brewster had higher hopes for it, noting that it had been invented "for the purposes of rational amusement." Though Brewster had patented the device, he made little money from it. The instrument was copied and marketed, selling in the thousands, before his own manufacturer could begin selling any.

Euphemism

A milder-sounding word or phrase used in place of something unpleasant or extreme-sounding.

....

The ancient Greeks gave us this word (*eu*, "good" + *pheme*, "speech") and also made good use of the technique themselves. Because they believed that to speak ill of the gods was to invoke their wrath, they were careful not to mention the gods by name. For example, they took to calling the Furies, a mythological trio of cruel, vengeful women, the Eumenides, or "Kindly Ones," even though in fact they were anything but kindly.

Gee, *gosh*, and *jeepers* all developed as alternatives to God and Jesus so that speakers would not profane holy names. *Casket* came into use in the mid-1800s to avoid the unpleasant associations of *coffin*. We teach children to say number one and number two instead of more explicit names for bodily functions. Over time, even some euphemisms come to be replaced with other euphemisms. For example, *lame* gave way to *crippled*, which in turn yielded to *handicapped* or *disabled*.

At its extreme, euphemism turns into doublespeak, in which language is used for political purposes to distort or disguise meaning. The business world is a prolific generator of euphemism. Layoffs becomes downsizing, for example.

MARCH 1

Mellifluous

The quality of smoothness, sweetness, or richness.

If a human voice is honey-sweet, we call it *mellifluous*. The Latin *mel* means "honey," and *fluus* means "flowing." So a mellifluous voice literally sounds like honey flowing. The word is an early 15th-century borrowing from Latin. English has a few other sweet words with honey lurking in them: *caramel, marmalade, molasses,* and *mousse. Melittology* is the study of bees.

MARCH 2

Ambulance

A vehicle whose purpose is to transport sick or injured people.

Ambul- is a combining form (a root that cannot occur on its own but rather must attach to an affix) that refers to motion. It comes from the Latin *ambulare*, meaning "to walk, travel." The world of medicine, never shy about adapting Latin, has made good use of the root, as a number of the words formed from it have a medical sense. Patients who are not confined to a bed—those able to walk—are *ambulatory*. Sometimes it's not the patients that are moving, but the hospital. The French *hôpital ambulant*, or "walking hospital," eventually became our *ambulance*. There is an old sense of *ambulant* that describes a disease that moves from one part of the body to another. And there is the seemingly oxymoronic *ambulatorium*, literally "walking place," used to refer to a dispensary or outpatient clinic.

Gargoyle

A grotesquely carved figure, typically found projecting from the top edge of a building.

Most would agree that *gargoyle* is not the prettiest word in English, which is fitting, as gargoyles are strange and ugly carvings of people or animals, usually attached to gutters to carry rainwater away from buildings. (Gargoyles were originally used in the 13th century to keep water from running down the walls of buildings and eroding the mortar holding the stones together.)

The word comes from the Old French *gargouille* ("throat"), and most gargoyles spout water through their throats. (Other words related to gargoyle are *gargle*, *gurgle*, and *gullet*—they all ultimately originated from a Greek word meaning "to gargle.") Because the functionality of gargoyles requires that they extend a good length from the building in order for the water to drain properly, they are usually exaggerated and bizarre representations of people and animals—typically monkeys, dogs, lions, snakes, wolves, or eagles. It's common for one gargoyle to combine several different creatures—you'll see harpies, griffins, and mermaids featured. These gargoyles are called chimeras.

Mitzvah

Jewish rabbinical commandment; an act of charity or human kindness in keeping with Jewish law.

Mitzvah originally referred to any one of the 613 commandments Jews are expected to follow, but since most of them have to do with being kind to others, it has come to mean "a good deed." "Helping that man across the street was a mitzvah." A *bar mitzvah* is a ceremony held at a synagogue when a Jewish boy turns 13. The term literally means "son of the commandment" and signifies that the boy is now old enough to understand the religious laws and is making the transition to adulthood and adult responsibilities. A *bat mitzvah* is a similar ceremony held for 12-year-old girls. Sources indicate that these ceremonies began to be observed in the Middle Ages.

The Hebrew word literally means "commandment, precept," and comes from *tziwwah* ("he commanded"). Its first use is in Genesis 26:5, where God says, "Because that Abraham obeyed my voice, and kept my charge, my commandments, my statutes, and my laws."

Juggernaut

Something massive and nearly unstoppable; a force that defeats everything in its path.

....

The versatile *juggernaut* can be applied to many things. Television shows with huge ratings are referred to as juggernauts. Extremely successful sports teams are juggernauts. Popular internet fixtures like Facebook are juggernauts. Despite such versatility, the origin of this word is rather opaque. It evolved from the Hindi word *Jagannath*, a combination of *jagat* ("world") and *natha* ("lord, protector"). In Hinduism, the word refers to Krishna, the eighth incarnation of the religion's supreme deity, Vishnu. Every year in the Indian city of Puri, an idol of this deity is hauled in a procession on a huge, elaborately decorated chariot or car. This public spectacle sounds so memorable, that it's no wonder the English word it spawned stayed firmly planted in the lexicon.

Although the word has semantically broadened, juggernaut's two subtly different figurative senses are both nods to powerful mayhem. In reference to the actual vehicle, there is juggernaut as inexorable force. Another sense, that of something—an institution, movement, notion, or practice—that elicits blind and often destructive devotion, relies more heavily on the word's idol-worshipping lineage.

Apocalypse

A disastrous event causing destruction, upheaval, or loss.

....

Apocalypse comes from the Latin *apocalypsis* and is ultimately from the Greek *apokalypsis* (*apo*, "off " and *kalyptein*, "to cover"), meaning "disclosure" or "revelation." The *Apocalypsis Ioannis* (*Book of the Revelation of St. John*) is the final book of the Vulgate Latin Bible and provides a vision of the end of time.

For centuries the word apocalypse was used in English to only refer to *Book of the Revelation of St. John*. But at the end of the 19th century, people began using apocalypse to describe the events in that biblical book or any cataclysm that necessitated the destruction of the world or life as we know it. An apocalpyse became any major catastrophe. And much more recently, the element -*calypse* has become separated and applied to all sorts of calamitous events. An etymologist would not rate -*calypse* as a likely candidate for a productive suffix, but that hasn't stopped inventive wordsmiths from using the two syllables as a suffix in a variety of nonce words and humorous coinages. For example, *apopcalypse* (destruction of Western civilization by the evils of popular culture), *aquacalypse* (damage to the sea from overfishing), or even *Grandmacalypse* (a visit from a relative who spoils the kids, and the attendant destruction of discipline).

Philtrum

The vertical groove above the middle of the upper lip.

....

Who even knew there was a word for this? The word *phil-trum* derives from the ancient Greek term *philtron*, which means "love potion." Although the philtrum may seem inconsequential to modern humans, the ancient Greeks believed it to be one of the most erogenous parts of the human body. English contains other little-used words for very specific parts of the body, for example: *supercilium* (the region of the eyebrows), *thrapple* (the throat, specifi-cally related to the windpipe), *pinna* (the outward portion of the ear), *popliteal space* (an oblong region behind and below the knee), and *hallux* (big toe).

Ugly

Disagreeable or offensive, especially to the sight.

....

Ugly is an old and much-used word with a history stretch-ing back at least to the 13th century. The word probably comes from a Scandinavian source, like the Old Norse *ug-gligr* ("fearful, dreadful"). It may be related to *agg* ("strife"). In early usage, the word was restricted to more extreme contexts, as in something dire or terrifying. Over time, the definition softened to include "unpleasant to look at" or "morally repugnant."

Jazz

An American musical form that grew out of several musical traditions, including ragtime and the blues, at the beginning of the 1900s; characterized by flexible syncopation, improvisation, and complex chords.

....

Jazz can hold a variety of meanings, depending on who's doing the talking. It has obscure roots in 19th-century American slang. A commonly accepted word history (though not the only one) has it arising in California, specifically in relation to baseball sports writing. In this context, its first known appearance was in 1912, and meant something like "peppy, energetic." In a matter of years, it was being used in association with a specific kind of music in Chicago and New Orleans. As that form of music grew in popularity, the word's meaning constricted. As a verb, we might still "jazz" something up, but as a noun, the word means the homegrown musical form now known all over the world. That initial intangible quality of something vital, spirited, and full of life has stuck with the word ever since.

Hyperbole

A conscious overstatement of facts for dramatic or comedic effect.

Hyperbole, like most rhetorical terms, comes to us from ancient Greek, and back then it meant pretty much what it means in English today: excess or exaggeration. It's often used in everyday speech, such as when we refer to someone as "older than dirt" or say, "this box weighs a ton." "I'm so hungry I could eat a horse!" is another common example. Any time we exaggerate to make something seem worse—or better ("I feel like a million bucks")—than it really is, we're using hyperbole.

Hyperbole—both the word and the rhetorical device—has been used for a very long time. The Greek philosopher Aristotle stated that hyperbole has a "juvenile character" and is most often used by people when they are angry (or vehement). Shakespeare used it in *Macbeth* in Lady Macbeth's famous line, "all the perfumes of Arabia will not sweeten this little hand," and so have many other authors, down to the present day.

MARCH 11

Sabotage

Deliberate destruction of an object or hampering of a process or goal.

Sabotage came to us from French around the year 1907, and carried with it the sense of a bungled endeavor, or something done poorly. Along the way, it acquired the sense of *purposeful* bungling. *Saboter* ("to sabotage, walk noisily") is from *sabot* ("wooden shoe"). It was typically used to refer to an act of destruction of an employer's property by workers. After being used in World War I to describe clandestinely inflicted damage in military contexts, its meaning broadened.

MARCH 12

Garbage

Material considered useless; rubbish or trash.

Garbage was probably one of a number of cookery-related words that came to us from Anglo-French. Usage roughly appeared in the mid-16th century. It specifically had to do with the waste parts of an animal, but broadened to include kitchen refuse in general. By the end of that century it had already come to include any worthless or waste material. It can now be used to describe immaterial things like art, ideas, songs, or opinions.

Chronogram

A form of wordplay in which the letters used in a sentence or phrase describing an event correspond to numerals signifying the date of the event.

....

The word *chronogram* literally means "time writing." It derives from the Greek words *chronos* and *gramma*, or "time" and "letter." To produce a chronogram, you might take the year of the event, convert it into Roman numerals, and compose a sentence describing the event that includes letters equivalent to those Roman numerals. For instance, you could write a sentence in which all the letters that can double as Roman numerals are added together to achieve the desired sum. All such letters must be used—no extraneous I's or V's left over at the end. One might commemorate 2008 with the sentence ELECTION DAY CARRIES BARACK OBAMA TO OVAL OFFICE, which whittles down to

L + C + I + D + C + I + C +M + V + L + I + C = 50 + 100 + 1 + 500 + 100 + 1 + 100 + 1,000 + 5 +50 + 1 + 100 = 2008.

This sort of chronogram originated in the Roman Empire but was particularly common during the European Renaissance.

Migraine

A moderate to severe recurrent headache, especially on one side of the head, that may last from several hours to several days; associated with light or sound sensitivity, nausea, or vomiting.

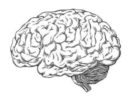

This French borrowing came into English meaning much the same as it does now. It is derived from the Latin *hemicrania* ("pain in one part of the head"), which comes from a similar Greek word. It's no wonder there's a dedicated word for this affliction—*migraines* can be downright horrible for some sufferers. The recent coinage *migraineur* denotes anyone who suffers from the affliction.

BEAR IN MIND

The causes of migraines aren't completely understood, but one theory that has gained traction focuses on brain cells. Waves of activity by groups of excitable brain cells trigger chemicals like serotonin. These chemicals narrow blood vessels throughout the body. A migraine results.

A cognate word, *megrim*, was once used to describe the same condition. Though no longer in common usage, the word may also be used to describe low spirits, dizziness, vertigo, and whims or fancies.

Skedaddle

To flee, especially in a chaotic or unplanned manner.

This word's origin is murky at best. According to Michael Quinion in the e-magazine *World Wide Words*, *skedaddle* became popular during the Civil War. The original usage specifically pointed to a sudden retreat from battle, but it quickly made its way into civilian speech and print. Its first appearance in print, in the *New York Tribune* (1861), suggests not just retreat but a cowardly one at that: "No sooner did the traitors discover their approach than they 'skiddaddled,' (a phrase the Union boys up here apply to the good use the seceshers make of their legs in time of danger)."

However it came about, skedaddle is a delightfully fun collection of letters, with sound symbolism both ahead and behind. The *sk-* reminds us of *skip, scoot, scram, scuttle,* and *scatter.* The verb *to addle* means "to make confused or disoriented"; the same final sound is found in muddle and befuddle. Put the meanings together, and you can almost guess the meaning of skedaddle just from how it sounds.

MARCH 16

Pickle

A brine or vinegar solution used to preserve food; often referring to a specific vegetable, like cucumbers, prepared in this manner.

Pickle probably comes from the Middle Dutch *pekel*, a word that has relatives in other Germanic languages. When it entered English in the early 1400s, it meant "spiced sauce," something that was served with or on a meat dish. The specific association with cucumbers dates to 1707. By the mid-16th century, it had extended to mean something like "in a state of difficulty," a sense that is still with us ("in a pickle").

MARCH 17

Orange

The round, rind-covered fruit of the orange tree; the color typically represented by the fruit.

The simple, everyday word *orange* has traveled through many languages, just as the fruit has traveled through many lands. The tree's original range was probably restricted to northern India, and from here we derive the Sanskrit source word *naranga-s*. It entered Persian as *narang*, and Arabic as *naranj*. Trade brought the fruit to Italy, where it became *narancia* and then *arancia*. By the time it first arrived in English via French, it was *orenge*.

Circuit

A line encompassing an area, typically circular.

....

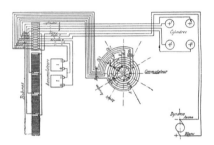

The possible definitions for *circuit* are now robust, but when the word entered English in the late 14th century, it simply meant the definition we give here. The Old French source word emphasized its sense as a journey. The Latin *circuitus* means "going around," and *circum* means "round." From the 1400s, it acquired the sense of "space enclosed within limits." Along the way, the word became associated with the practice of journeying from one place to another to perform a task or duty, like a musical performance or judicial assignment (think "Chitlin' Circuit" or "circuit judge"). One of its most frequent uses now is in relation to electronics as "a complete path of an electric current or an assemblage of electronics components." This sense draws from a definition that came into being in the 1740s ("an assembly of equipment that allows a current to be kept between two poles"). This sense has seeped into organic applications and the word is now applied to neuronal pathways of the brain along which signals may travel.

Harvest

The time of year when a cultivated crop is gathered; the activity of gathering crops.

The Old English word *hærfest* meant "autumn." This word derives from Proto-Germanic and has plenty of cognate words in other Germanic languages: German *herbst*, Dutch *herfst*, Old Norse *haust*, and Old Saxon *hervist*, for example. The Proto-Indo-European root *kerp* ("to pluck, gather") also gives us *carpet, excerpt, scarcity* and is part of the Latin phrase *carpe diem*.

The Old English word denoting the season between August and November only incidentally indicated the activity of gathering crops. By the mid-13th century, a semantic shift had occurred and the word was taking modern shape. Meanwhile, the borrowed *autumn* and repurposed *fall* stepped in to denote the season. Figurative uses for the word began in the 16th century.

MARCH 20

Enigma

Something or someone that is inscrutable or difficult to understand.

GET CRACKING

The Enigma machine was a cipher device used by the German military in World War II to send coded messages. It was considered too complex to crack. However, Allied researchers did crack it eventually, a feat which shortened the duration of the war.

The word *enigma* entered English in the 1530s with the restricted meaning of any phrase that composed a riddle or was somehow complicated or obscure. This sense comes from Latin and Greek terms that also denoted verbal riddles. By extension, it later came to be applied to things and people.

MARCH 21

Triage

Assigning a priority order, primarily in a medical scenario, of who or what to attend to, for the purpose of obtaining the best result.

In medicine, *triage* is the process of deciding which patients should receive attention and care first, based on the relative seriousness of their conditions. As a practice, the system began to evolve within the French military at the end of the 18th century. It was a highly effective system for minimizing casualties, and the practice saw widespread adoption during World War I.

Environment

The conditions or circumstances surrounding something or someone.

. . . .

This is a rather broad and vaguely put definition, but the word has grown to encompass so many possible scenarios that it almost functions as a catch-all word, like *thing*. The root *environ* (from the Old French *environer*) denotes encirclement or a sense of enclosure. This word contained the root *virer* ("to turn"), which is related to our *veer*.

MARCH 23

Aplomb

Doing something with the appearance of competence; presenting a confident demeanor.

. . . .

A PLUM FACT

. . . .

What does a *plumber* do? Most people won't say *plumb*, but that is the source for the word. This verb comes from the noun of the same spelling. As a noun, it referred to a piece of lead hung on a string to show a vertical line.

This French word entered English in 1828 and immediately had the sense of "self-possession" it has today. It was derived from *à plomb* ("balanced," or "on the plumb line"). If *aplomb* seems similar to *plumber*, that's because the words share a similar Latin root, *plumbum* ("lead," the metal).

Innuendo

An allusion or insinuation, usually indirect, that suggests an impropriety or something questionable about the subject being referred to.

Medieval legal documents first used the Latin *innuendo* with the sense of "that is to say" or "to wit." The term was used to introduce parenthetical or explanatory remarks. The classical Latin *innuere* meant "to nod toward, or make a sign to" a person—something like giving a hint. The definition gradually broadened to any kind of indirect suggestion, with derogatory aspects coming to predominate.

The venerable practice of innuendo in literature is as old as Shakespeare and has continued into the present (think Monty Python). Ending a phrase with "if you know what I mean" is an example of conversational innuendo. Marx Brothers films are filled with it. In the classic, *Monkey Business*, Madame Swempski tells Groucho, "I don't like this innuendo." He replies, "Well, it's like I always say: Love goes out the door when money comes innuendo."

Clerihew

A short, humorous poetic form consisting of four lines of no fixed length or rhythm, with the rhyme scheme AABB, which tells a mini story about a famous person (whose name typically appears as, or in, the first line of the poem).

The *clerihew* derives its name from its creator, English novelist and humorist Edmund Clerihew Bentley. This poem is not expected to be factual or informative in any way, and the more awkward the rhythm, the better. For instance, here is a famous one by Bentley himself:

Sir Christopher Wren
Said, "I am going to dine with some men.
If anybody calls,
Say I am designing St. Paul's."

The style is evocative of Ogden Nash, though the form predates his work. Bentley's first collection of light verse, *Biography for Beginners*, was published in 1905, when Nash was only three years old. It's unknown whether Ogden Nash took any inspiration from clerihews; he never wrote any, as far as anyone knows. But others did—for instance, W. H. Auden. However, the most prolific writer of clerihews was Edmund Clerihew Bentley himself.

Martinet

A strict or pedantic person who demands rigid adherence to protocols and procedures.

Lieutenant Colonel Jean Martinet was appointed inspector general of King Louis XIV's infantry in the late 17th century. As such, he was responsible for enforcing drill protocol and discipline. The king's drillmaster proved a genius at training troops in precision maneuvers. Specifically, he trained them to move in precise formations and to fire musket volleys only on command. This had the effect of making the notoriously inaccurate muskets much more effective in battle. The result was noticeable; the revamped French army showed superior discipline, prowess, and accuracy on the battlefield. The English took note of the results. Awareness of the French officer who had goaded his troops into following strict discipline and following the smallest details of protocol percolated among English officers. The surname became synonymous with the practice. Used this way, the word's first known recorded use in print appeared in 1779. *Martinet* is an example of an *eponym*, a word coined from a person's name.

MARCH 27

Pruinose

Being covered with a white powder or bloom or appearing frosted, typically in relation to botany.

....

Pruinose is a wonderfully specialized and poetic word. Unfortunately, there aren't too many contexts in which to use it. A frosty autumn lawn or winter windowpane might be called pruinose. Alternately, freezer-burnt meat or a moldy piece of fruit could be described the same way. The word comes from the Latin *pruinosus* ("frosted") and has been used in English (albeit rarely) since 1818.

MARCH 28

Schlimazel

Someone who attracts misfortune or is chronically unlucky or inept.

....

A word that's fun to say but not so fun to be, *schlimazel* comes to us from a Yiddish phrase *shlim mazel* meaning "bad luck." It was being used in English by 1948. The origin words are the Middle High German *slim* ("crooked") and the Hebrew *mazzal* ("luck"). Anyone with a memory that extends back to 70s sitcoms will remember the word appearing in a nonsense phrase sung by the two main characters in *Laverne & Shirley*'s theme song : "Schlemiel! Schlimazel! Hasenpfeffer Incorporated!"

Kakistocracy

Government by the worst people.

Kakistocracy appeared in English in the 17th century as a coinage of uncertain origin. It comes from two root words: the Greek *kakistos* ("worst") and the word-forming element *-cracy* (from Latin by way of French *-cratie*, which refers to governmental rule). If the front part of the word looks like it might be related to *caca* ("excrement"), a foreign word that now has a colloquial status in English, that's because it is; both words trace back to the Proto-Indo-European *kakka* ("to defecate").

MARCH 30

Zombie

A human body reanimated by supernatural means.

The *Oxford English Dictionary* says the word *zombie* is of obscure western and central African origin and compares it to the African words *nzambi* ("god") and *zumbi* ("fetish"). In 1940, *Time* magazine said that W. B. Seabrook's book *The Magic Island*, a fictional account of voodoo cults in Haiti, "introduced 'zombi' into U.S. speech." Zombies were permanently put on the map of horror lore by the 1968 film *Night of the Living Dead*.

Nun

A female member of a religious order.

....

Sometimes the simplest words have the richest or strangest word histories. The Old English *nunne* had much the same meaning as it does now—"a woman who adheres to a specific religious life." The word would have been restricted to Christianity by English speakers of the time, but usage extends back to the pagan practices of Rome. It might have referred to a vestal or pagan priestess. In those times, the feminine *nonna* and masculine *nonnus* might also be used as terms of address for elders. Underlying these historical uses is a word that occurs over and over in Proto-Indo-European and has to do with a woman seen in the context of a specific relationship to others. So, there is the Italian *nonna* and Welsh *nain* ("grandmother"), the Greek *nanna* ("aunt"), the Croation *nena* ("mother"), and the Persian *nana* ("mother"). Our modern *nanny* comes from the same source.

Choleric

Hot-tempered, quick to anger.

If you find yourself easily angered when things go wrong, you might be called *choleric*. This term goes back to ancient Greek medicine. They believed that imbalances in any of four metabolic agents in the human body (known as humours) explained various maladies. The four humours were the *sanguine* (blood), *phlegmatic* (phlegm), *melancholic* (black bile), and *choleric* (yellow bile). When a humour became imbalanced, it could lead to certain observable conditions. In the case of a choleric imbalance, the result was frequently anger.

Anathema

Someone or something deeply detested, the subject of ban, curse, or excommunication.

The semantic weight of *anathema* may have lightened in recent usage, but its medieval ecclesiastical meaning was "an excommunicated or cursed person." Anathema was not a casual term in the Catholic Church. By the 20th century, a deeply disliked opinion, belief, or practice could be called anathema. Casual contemporary usage continues to chip away at its intensity, and the word appears to be going the way of *awful*.

Satellite

A celestial object, manmade or otherwise, orbiting another object.

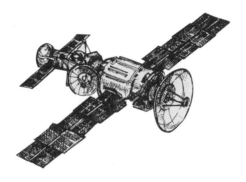

When speaking of *satellites*, most people mean one thing: those shiny things we put in orbit around the Earth. This brings us to an important point: that science fiction authors with their heads in the clouds do more than write entertaining stories. They help us create the future. In 1945, the writer Arthur C. Clarke published a proposal in *Wireless World*. He outlined the idea of positioning a communications device in geosynchronous orbit. He described this device as an "artificial satellite." He took his term from a word that already existed: in astronomy, a satellite was a celestial body like a moon orbiting another larger body. In this sense, the word had been used by astronomers going back to Johannes Kepler in the early 17th century. Today we take the information beamed to us from satellites for granted—a magical convenience of the modern age. Which brings us something else Clarke said: "Any sufficiently advanced technology is indistinguishable from magic."

APRIL 4

Ichnolite

The fossilized impression of a footprint.

....

The field of archaeology is the repository of a number of necessary coinages, and *ichnolite* is a fun result of this need. The word began to be used in the field in the 1840s. It only means one thing: those amazing footprints that were somehow captured in the fossil record. *Ichnite* means the same thing, and *ichnology* refers to the study of fossil footprints. The root Greek word, *ikhnos*, means "track, footprint."

APRIL 5

Katabatic

A kind of cold, dense wind that flows down from higher elevations, like the side of a glacier or mountain.

....

This loan word is from the Greek *katabasis* or *katabainein* ("to go down"), a compound from *kata* ("down") and *banein* ("to go, walk"). Katabatic wind is also known as drainage or fall wind because it will carry high-density winds downslope by force of gravity. The phenomena is memorable and some katabatic winds are famous. The mistral winds of southern France blow down river valleys and out into the Mediterranean. The Santa Ana winds blow out to sea from southern California's interior. The bora winds of the northern Adriatic are famous for their occasional hurricane intensity.

Luxury

Wealth, splendor, opulence.

Today we associate the word *luxury* with material goods, but when the word first entered English it meant "sexual desire," or "lust." It was borrowed from French around 1340. It is ultimately from the Latin *luxuria*, meaning "extravagance, excess,"  a word the ancient Romans used to emphasize excessive waste. A milder term that meant simply "wealth, splendor" was the word *luxus*. By the time the Latin *luxuria* had filtered down into Norman-French, it had taken on the sexual meaning, and it was this meaning that was adopted into English and persisted for a few hundred years, lasting from Middle English through the beginnings of modern English.

Use of luxury in the sense we use it today appeared in the early 17th century, meaning it existed alongside the "lascivious" sense for a century or so. Since this modern English sense is closer to the original Latin meaning, it is probably the result of people reinterpreting the word to reflect the old meaning. Most literate people of the time also knew Latin and would have been familiar with how classical writers used the word. It is this sense that survives today.

Metonymy

A rhetorical device that replaces one thing with something closely associated with it.

....

Metonymy comes from an ancient Greek word meaning "change of name." That comes pretty close to explaining the function of metonymy today. Common examples of metonymy include using "Washington" to refer to the U.S. government, or "the Crown" to refer to the English government. As the United States' capital city and the location where most federal business takes place, Washington is so intrinsically associated with the government that it functions nominally as a stand-in.

Metonymy can work in two directions: A larger thing can represent a smaller thing, or a smaller thing can represent a larger thing. For example, when a headline declares "White House Reports One Million Jobs Lost," obviously the building itself is not doing the reporting. Rather, someone who works in the building has reported the losses. But people also use "the White House" to mean the entirety of the executive branch of the U.S. government (not just those who work in the building itself). When headlines blare "Congress Battles White House Over Reform," for example, it's not just the workers from one building who are fighting, but the entire executive branch.

Wring

To twist and squeeze something, usually to get liquid out of it.

. . . .

Wring is one of those odd words, like *wrong, wreck,* and *wrestle,* that has a silent *w* before the *r*. This is a case of fossilized spelling. Several centuries ago, the *w* was pronounced. The pronunciation has changed over time, but the spelling, preserved in written records, remains.

What you typically wring is something made of cloth. You might occasionally be tempted to wring someone's neck, but you must of course resist, lest their loved ones wring justice from you. That last usage ("wring justice") points to a figurative sense, "to extract something with effort," as when you "wring meaning" from a difficult text.

DON'T WRING ME UP

. . . .

You may never have seen an old-fashioned washing machine equipped with a *wringer,* operated with a crank, but such devices were once common. Wet clothes were cranked through the wringer to squeeze excess water out of them before they were hung up to dry. The technology is gone, but we still sometimes put someone "through the wringer" when we want to squeeze information or action out of them.

Jejune

Lifeless, dull, devoid of interest; childish or immature.

Jejune is most commonly used as a putdown word in English. To describe an adult's actions, attitude, or comments as jejune is to take them down a notch and perhaps suggest a hint of immaturity. A shallow or undeveloped taste in art or music might be described as jejune, for example.

The Latin borrowing (from *ieiunus,* "empty, barren) was being used in English in the early 17th century. Previous to that, it appeared in medical literature as *jejunum.* The source word's ultimately origin is obscure. The word's earliest meaning emphasized "empty or meager" in a more concrete, less judgmental sense.

SOMETHING TO DIGEST

Jejunum is the medical anatomy term for a section of the small intestine. The choice of the Latin derivative was due to the fact that this part of the intestine was typically found empty during dissection.

Pandemic

Occurring over a large area (as in multiple countries), typically referring to a disease that affects a large part of a population.

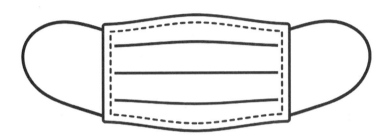

To the surprise of no one, Merriam-Webster's Word of the Year in 2020 was *pandemic*. The dictionary's website revealed a jump in lookups for the word beginning that January, coinciding with the first positive case in the United States. A significant spike came on February 3, the day the first COVID-19 patient was allowed to leave a hospital in Seattle. The spike didn't fall off—rather, lookups continued. In March, the World Health Organization announced that COVID-19 could be described as a pandemic. This led to the biggest spike of all: a whopping 115,806% increase compared to the previous year! Can a single word really define an entire year? Perhaps not usually, but it's hard to argue with the 2020 selection.

The word has been around for much longer, of course. "Pandemic disease" traces at least to the 1850s. The word is taken from the Latin *pandemus,* and is built from *pan* ("all") and *demos* ("people").

Pumpernickel

A dark and coarse bread made with whole rye grain.

In a contest involving words that are fun to say, *pumpernickel* might or might not be considered a frontrunner. But in a contest involving fun etymologies, the word would definitely be a winner. The word is German in origin. The first part, *pumpern*, is an old word that typically meant "breaking wind." The second part, *nickel*, had multiple connotations, having to do with goblins, demons, and all-around rascals. It came from the proper name *Niklaus*, a frequent euphemism for the Devil (as in "Old Nick"). So how does a word for a type of bread come to signify something like "devil farts"? Well, the bread did have a very high fiber content, and could have led to problems of indigestion and flatulence, and thus got its name that way. One supportable conjecture has the word catching on at the end of the Thirty Years' War, with soldiers stationed in the Westphalia region of Germany complaining about the effects of the local dark peasant bread that was part of their rations. It's a reasonable—and fun—conjecture, but still is only speculation.

Kahuna

An important personage, a bigwig.

....

Kahuna comes to English from the Hawaiian language, and originally was used to refer to an expert in a field, like a priest, doctor, navigator, or general healer. Expert craftsmen, like canoe builders, might also be called kahunas. A Hawaiian governmental report from 1886 defines a kahuna as a "doctor and sorcerer." The word caught on in surfer slang in the 1960s. As it began circulating in American English, its sense broadened, coming to mean anyone who holds a position of power or importance.

APRIL 13

Heliotrope

A plant of the genus *Heliotropium*, part of the borage family.

....

Specialized botanical terms like *heliotrope* often contain fascinating roots that teach us about English words in general. *Helio* is from a Greek word meaning "sun." *Trope* ("a turn, change") is the source of a number of English words, like *contrive, entropy, retrieve, tropic,* and *troubadour.* The word heliotrope, as a "plant which turns to follow the sun," is perfectly evocative. That said, heliotropism is common among other flowers, and figuratively one could say that even certain people are heliotropic.

Obstreperous

Obnoxious, noisy, or clamorous, in an unruly or stubborn way.

Children seem to be frequently described as *obstreperous*, in the sense that they can present a formidably willful anarchy to the adults attempting to keep control of them. It's a word perfectly suited for the job. Along with children, adults and animals can be obstreperous too. For example, a crowd clashing with police during a political protest might be described as obstreperous. A mule that loudly decides it isn't going to go where someone wants it to go could also be called obstreperous.

The Latin *obstreperus* means "clamorous." The root *ob-* means "across, against" and *strepere* means "to make noise." Words with the root *ob-* abound in English and often carry the sense of conflict or opposition with them. For example: *object, obnoxious, obstacle, obstinate, obstruct,* and *oppress.*

Grok

To grasp something deeply and intuitively.

Grok is now an unknown word to most people, but it did enjoy use, at least by young people, in the 1960s. Robert Heinlein's science fiction novel *Stranger in a Strange Land* was published in 1961. In his novel, the protagonist is a human who was born on Mars and was raised by Martians. As a young adult, he comes to Earth. He brings with him the language of the Martians. Among the words he uses is grok, an arbitrary Heinlein coin-

age. The word was deeply significant in the novel, and served to underpin the difference between Earth and Martian outlooks. At one point in the novel, grok is described this way: "Grok means to understand so thoroughly that the observer becomes a part of the observed—to merge, blend, intermarry, lose identity in group experience." Science fiction enthusiasts of the time, especially in youth culture, were attracted to the idea of deeply and empathically understanding something (as an example of desirable higher-than-human sentience) and were soon peppering their conversation with the word.

Tyro

Someone new or just beginning to learn; a newbie.

Tyro comes from the Latin *tiro*, a word that similarly meant "beginner, new recruit." As an all-purpose word for novices and newbies, it has been freely used since the early 17th century, especially by writers. Herman Melville called men newly recruited to whaling ships tyros: "As she slowly drew nigh, from my lofty perch at the fore-mast-head, I had a good view of that sight so remarkable to a tyro in the far ocean fisheries—a whaler at sea, and long absent from home."

There is an entire roster of words in English that give us overlapping definitions of the same thing: *acolyte, amateur, apprentice, babe, beginner, colt, cub, dilettante, fledgling, freshman, greenhorn, neophyte, newcomer, novice, novitiate, punk, recruit, rookie, tenderfoot, virgin.* English speakers apparently like having a robust offering of words that can be used to describe those who have less experience or expertise than themselves.

Wonk

Someone who specializes in, or is preoccupied by, arcane details and procedures.

Overly studious bookworms, lovers of tediously fine detail, and specialists in obscure esoterica can all be called *wonks*. It's not an inherently pejorative word, but the label does often carry a stigma, as if the so-designated party's attitudes or practices are somehow problematic. *Policy wonk* often carries the same negative connotation that *bureaucrat* does.

The word may have derived from one of two other words—*wonky* ("unstable, shaky"), another word of uncertain origin, or *wanker* ("masturbator, contemptible person"), British slang of uncertain origin.

The word has always had negative connotations. It has been in usage since about 1954. By the end of that decade, it carried the sense of "effeminate male." In the 1980s, Ivy League slang influenced its meaning, and it came to be blurred with that of *nerd*. In current American usage, it is almost always used in the context of those professionals who have expertise in government policy.

Oxymoron

A figure of speech that contains a combination of contradictory words.

....

The word comes from the Greek *oxus,* meaning "sharp," and *moros,* "foolish"—so the word itself is oxymoronic. The oxymoron is an arresting figure of speech, demonstrating the power of the imaginative mind to discover similarities and correspondences even among opposites. Traditionally, the term refers to that discovery of similarities, of something surprisingly true, and not to a mere contradiction.

For example, the computer term *fuzzy logic* is a deliberate oxymoron. It refers to logical reasoning about conditions that can be "sort of" true or false. The oxymoron is used to highlight how different this is from traditional computer logic, which works in black and white, not shades of gray.

Many oxymorons—most commonly in adjective-noun combinations—have become commonplace: *silent scream, deafening silence, sweet sorrow, open secret, jumbo shrimp, only choice, old news, civil war, virtual reality*—even *bittersweet.* Often, oxymorons are used deliberately and ironically, as in "that's a definite maybe," or "I think she did it accidentally on purpose."

Epiplexis

A rhetorical technique in which the speaker tries to persuade the audience by chiding them.

....

Epiplexis (from the Greek *plessein,* "to strike") often takes the form of a rhetorical question, in which someone suggests something in the form of a question for which no answer is expected. With epiplexis, the speaker reproaches the audience not to plunge them into shame but to goad them into action.

Writing in 1798 about regional and sectional frictions in the new republic, Thomas Jefferson asked his countrymen: "If to rid ourselves of the present rule of Massachusetts and Connecticut, we break the Union, will the evil stop there? Suppose the New England States alone cut off, will our nature be changed? Are we not men still to the south of that, and with all the passions of men?"

Epiplexis is perhaps not so gentle in all cases. "How could you have been so stupid?" is obviously not uttered to get an answer to the literal question, but instead to goad the listener into agreeing with the speaker rather than appear dim-witted. Parents, especially, excel at this kind of rhetorical strategy: "Aren't you ashamed of yourself? I thought you were smarter than that."

Jape

Action meant jokingly or to arouse amusement.

Perhaps from the Old French *japer* ("to scream or bawl"), *jape* came into English in the late 14th century. It enjoyed moderate use in literary works from that century, but fell into disuse for some time. Then, in the 19th century, writers looking for a word meaning "jeer or jest" rediscovered the word. It has continued to show up in works of literature ever since and remains a literary word—but is not so common in everyday conversation.

Gibbous

Tending to swell; in astronomy, a moon or planet viewed with more than half of its disk illuminated.

We tend to come across the written phrase "gibbous moon" occasionally, but as applied to other objects ("gibbous camel," "gibbous flower"), *gibbous* is rarely seen. That's a shame—it's the perfect term for so many things—houses, hats, angry cats, and mysterious objects under blankets. It comes from a Latin word which means "hump" or "hump-backed."

Khaki

Light yellowish-brown; a light-colored cotton cloth.

....

Khaki comes from a Persian-sourced Urdu word that means "dusty, soil-colored" from *khak* ("dust"). The word first entered English via usage by the British cavalry in the mid-19th century, if not a little earlier. British troops stationed in India adopted a light local cloth of twilled linen or cotton that they came to refer to as khaki. Among other advantages, this material did not show dirt.

The cloth, with its muted, earthy color, was a perfect desert camouflage color, and was subsequently used by the British in the Boer Wars. From there, its use spread through the military, British and otherwise. The word kept its military connotations for decades, but civilian use of the cloth first began to appear in the U.S. after American troops returned home from the Spanish-American War in dusky twill military trousers. Khaki apparel became especially popular after World War II.

As pants, khakis were also called *chinos*, a word that comes from the Spanish phrase *pantalones chinos* ("Chinese pants"). The phrase arose because the cloth itself was often manufactured in China. American usage shortened the phrase to chinos.

Mania

A form of madness, often marked by an excessive desire for something.

....

The word *mania* comes from post-classical Latin and ultimately from Greek. It's often used as a suffix in a compound word to denote a particular kind of mania. Some *manias* are genuine illnesses, like *erotomania* ("extreme sexual desire"—1874) and *megalomania* ("delusions of power"—1885). But others are faddish and popular coinages. In the sense of a craze or fad (think *Beatlemania)* rather than as a mental illness, the usage dates back to the late 1600s.

Some of the other maniacal words, both serious and tongue-in-cheek, are:

- *bibliomania*—excessive enthusiasm for books (1734)
- *hydromania*—excessive craving for water (1793)
- *monomania*—compulsion or obsession relating to a single area (1815)
- *egomania*—morbid love of self (1825)
- *kleptomania*—compulsion to steal (1830)
- *pyromania*—compulsion to start fires (1842)
- *dipsomania*—alcoholism (circa 1843)
- *oenomania*—excessive enthusiasm for wine (1852)
- *arithmomania*—compulsion to count and per-form calculations (1890)
- *micromania*—delusion that one's body or a body part is abnormally small (1892)
- *oniomania*—compulsion to purchase things (1895)

Momentum

The inertia an object possesses—its mass times its velocity; a growing strength or force.

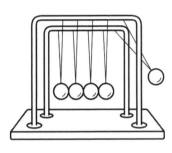

Momentum, originally meaning "a brief period of time," comes from Latin. In Anglo-Saxon England, a *momentum* was a fortieth of an hour—a minute and a half. The word took on a new meaning as our understanding of physics grew.

Isaac Newton's first law of motion tells us that objects at rest stay at rest and objects in motion stay in motion unless an external force is applied to them. An object with a lot of momentum is difficult to stop. In Newtonian physics, the force of an object's motion over an infinitesimally small period of time began to be called the object's momentum.

Today, we use the word most literally ("the car gathered momentum as it went down the hill") and figuratively ("the movie's box office sales gathered momentum with positive reviews"). And, of course, any politician tries to generate momentum in their campaign—sometimes by using a play on words. In 2004, for example, Connecticut senator Joe Lieberman coined the term *Joementum* to describe the supposedly unstoppable momentum that he had in the race for the Democratic presidential nomination.

Obloquy

Strong condemnation; the state of being condemned or discredited.

English has no shortage of stern, pejorative terms derived from Latin ecclesiastical sources. *Obloquy* is rarely used these days, but gives us yet another word focusing on contention, strife, and evil. The mid-15th century borrowing comes from *obloquium* ("speaking against, contradicting"). In case you're in need of more words to describe serious tongue-lashings, try these: *invective, vituperation, acrimony, vitriol, asperity, billingsgate,* or *abuse.*

APRIL 26

Metaphrastic

Translated or paraphrased; relating to verse translation.

A *metaphrast* is defined as one who adapts poetry or changes verse from one meter to another. As an adjective, *metaphrastic* has the sense of "close or word-by-word translation." It comes from the Greek *metaphrasis* ("paraphrase, translate"). Certainly it has always been a specialist term, but it's one of those words that could easily take on a broader, figurative sense. For example, we might critically note that some computer programmers have casual conversational styles that are metaphrastic while lauding certain journalists for their metaphrastic recall.

Troubadour

A poetic singer; historically, a lyric poet-musician of the Middle Ages.

Old Occitan, a Romance language once spoken across eastern Spain, southern France, and parts of Italy, gives us *troubadour*, a word that might have grown from *trobar* ("to find, to compose a song"), and which in turn might have come from the Latin *tropare* ("compose, sing") and *tropus* ("song"). An alternative etymology traces the word to the Latin *turbare* ("to dig up, disturb").

The famous poet-musicians known as troubadours were part of a flourishing court culture from the 11th to late 13th centuries. Thanks to the many written records that survive, we know that they often traveled from court to court, singing for the local aristocracy. Records of their songs survive too. They sang of many things—exotic faraway lands, gallant knights, faith and metaphysics, war, satire, trysts, betrayal—but were especially famous for songs about courtly love and chivalry, set in poetic structures characterized by intricate meter and rhyme.

SING FOR ME

The poetic culture of the troubadours had counterparts in other parts of Europe too. To the north were the French *trouveres*. And in Germany, the *minnesingers* also sang of courtly love, along with religion and social ideals.

89

Lute

A large, pear-shaped stringed instrument that was once commonly played in Europe.

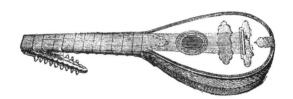

Anyone who has investigated the music of other cultures has probably noticed similarities between certain musical instruments. That's because they evolve into new forms over time, just as words change as they move into new languages. With the *lute*, we have an example of both.

The earliest European lute was based on an Arab instrument introduced into Spain in the 13th century. That instrument was known as the *ud* (now the *oud*). The Arabic phrase *al-ud* ("made of wood") simply became shortened; we find it becoming *lut* or *leut* in Old French later that century. While the oud only had four strings, the lute acquired more. By the mid-14th century, the strings had become pairs (known as *courses*). During the 15th century, frets were added to the fingerboard along with a fifth course. The European lute was at the height of its popularity in the 16th and 17th centuries.

The lute and the oud are now two distinct yet similar instruments, just as their names are.

Garble

Altered or distorted so as to change the meaning or make unintelligible.

You might say that semantically, *garble* is an example of itself. While its meaning has remained stable for several centuries, in former times it meant nearly the opposite of what it does now.

The Middle English word *garbelen* ("remove impurities") was borrowed from the Anglo-French *garbeler*, which in turn was borrowed from the Italian *garbellare*. These words were all used in roughly the same way, meaning "to sift through (spices) to remove impurities." Italian and other related Mediterranean languages all used a form of this word in the late Middle Ages. The source word was derived from the Arabic *gharbala* ("to sift, screen"). At the time, the spice trade was driving a linguistic exchange betweena number of languages around the Mediterranean and along trade routes. The Arabic word was a useful technical term that described the process of sifting and sieving spices and other botanicals to remove residuals like chaff. By the late 15th century, the verb, as it was used in English, had broadened its meaning to "remove what is objectionable."

Somehow during the next century, the core meaning was inverted. By the 1680s, it could mean "distort, mix up, confuse."

Scofflaw

One who proudly and defiantly breaks the law.

....

Scofflaw has its roots in the days of speakeasies and moonshine. The passing of the 18th Amendment made illegal the sale, manufacture, and transportation of alcohol for consumption. It also created a new kind of criminal, who brazenly flouted the new law. Noticing the absence of a word to characterize said lawbreakers, wealthy prohibitionist Delcevare King offered a $200 prize for the person who could come up with the best word to describe those who ignored the 18th Amendment. King received more than 25,000 entries, among them the word scofflaw—submitted by two separate contestants, Henry Irving Dale and Kate L. Butler. The word was selected as the winner, and the prize money was split evenly between them.

How Mr. Dale and Ms. Butler conjured up their winning word is clear enough. It's a combination of the verb

scoff, meaning "to mock or jeer," and *law*. The repeal of the 18th Amendment decriminalized the consumption of alcohol, but the word stuck around and expanded in scope, helped along by a New York City magistrate of the 1950s who used it for those who refused to pay traffic fines.

MAY 1

Sedulous

Carefully perseverant, diligent.

The Latin phrase *se dolus* ("without guile") was the source of *sedulus*, a word that came to mean "painstakingly diligent, zealous." This borrowing became the English *sedulous*. As we learned with *tyro* (a word with many synonyms), some concepts are robustly represented in the English vocabulary, and this is one of them. Other closely related words include *industrious, diligent, assiduous,* and *laborious.* It's important to be sedulous if you don't want to be a tyro.

MAY 2

Recondite

Difficult to understand; having to do with something obscure or poorly understood.

The English word *recondite* was borrowed in the early 17th century from the Latin *reconditus*, a word that means essentially the same thing. It's not a well-known or frequently-used word, but it's a very useful one, with plenty of real-world applications. For example, you might call the terms and conditions of that new app you downloaded recondite, along with computational neuroscience and quantum physics.

Idiot

Derogatory term for one who speaks or acts in a foolish, stupid, or nonsensical way.

In some ways, the word *idiot* has stayed remarkably consistent. The earliest meaning in the *Oxford English Dictionary*—"a person without learning; an ignorant, uneducated man; a simple man; a clown"—is not far from its contemporary sense. The word has its origins in the Greek *idiotes*, meaning "commoner" or "layman" and, hence, one who is ignorant or ill-informed. It came to English from the French *idiot* by way of the Latin *idiota,* which, similar to the Greek, means "an uneducated, ignorant person."

While staying on the same general thoroughfare, the term has gone down some interesting alleyways over the years. In some cases, it has named a profession, similar to a clown, fool, or jester (this sense inspired the term *idiot's hood*, a predecessor of dunce cap). In the not-so-distant past, the word functioned as a quasi-technical medical term, part of an IQ-based intelligence classification system that distinguished between levels of intellectual disability. This system was eventually recognized as insensitive and ableist, and fell out of use.

Bourgeois

The middle class of a society; qualities or values associated with this class.

....

This French word originally pertained only to town dwellers (note the similarity between *bourg-* and *burg,* a word meaning "town") or tradespeople living in urban areas. Later it grew to include the entire French middle class, eventually extending to include any group belonging to the economic middle rank. It entered English in the mid-16th century. It typically only meant "citizen of a town," during the 1600s. A century later, it was also being used to describe anything socially middle class in taste or manners.

The word acquired its negative connotations thanks to Marxist writings of the 19th century. It began to be associated with the most objectionable aspects of capitalism, like exploitation of the proletariat, preoccupation with status, affluence, and respectability, and any excessive attachment to material goods. The word continues to carry a connotation of overconcern with wealth and respectability.

CURB YOUR BLING

....

The pejorative sense of bourgeois is intensified in the slang derivative variously spelled *bougie, boujee, boozhy, boojie* (among others). It refers to anyone who flaunts their affluence and is regarded as snobby or elitist in some way.

Egregious

Extraordinary in a bad way.

....

Egregious comes from the Latin *ex* ("out") + *greg* or *grex* ("flock"), literally meaning "towering above the flock." The first known use was in the 1500s. Historically, the term was used to describe something "remarkable in a good sense, of distinguished, eminent personal qualities." Over time, however, the term experienced a fall from grace with a pejorative semantic shift. It's now used to refer to something that is notable in a bad way: egregious errors, egregious misconduct, and so forth.

MAY 6

Bagel

A round baked roll.

....

Not unexpectedly, this word is of Yiddish origin (*beygl*, 1919), although there's a surprise in its roots—it's from the Middle High German *boug* ("ring, bracelet"), related to *biogan* ("to bend"). One type of flattened *bagel* with sprinkled onion flakes is referred to as a *bialy*, a shortened form of Bialystok, a city in Poland. Bagels were considered somewhat exotic in parts of the United States until the 1970s and '80s, when they became mass produced and available at supermarkets throughout the country. Traditionally bagels are boiled before being baked.

Barmy

Frothy, bubbly, sudsy; exhibiting ridiculous behavior.

Barmy dates to the 1530s and probably derived from the earlier *barm*. That word refers to the foamy by-product that collected on top of malt liquor during the brewing process. Barm was used to leaven bread and initiate fermentation in new batches of liquor.

Initially barmy was only used as a description of the fermentation process. But the figurative sense of having "a frothy top," or "a head full of foam" as that might be applied to other people, was too good to resist. By the end of the 16th century, both liquids and people could be barmy, as the Scottish poet Alexander Mongomerie pointed out:

Hope puts that haste into your head,
Which boils your barmy brain.

Quick

Fast, swift.

··

The word *quick* did not always mean "fast." The word comes from the Old English *cwic*, meaning "alive." This sense of the word is still occasionally used, but outside of a few stock phrases like "the quick and the dead" (i.e., the living and the dead) and "cut to the quick" (i.e., seriously wound; a reference to living flesh and to cutting a nail down to the living tissue), it is pretty rare nowadays.

The original sense appears in the phrase "quick with child," meaning "pregnant." The word *quickening*, once common but now quite rare, refers to the first movements of a fetus in the womb. The original meaning also survives in *quicksilver* (another name for mercury), a word that goes back to the Old English *cwicseolfor* and is a reference to the fact that drops of mercury move as if they're alive.

Around the year 1300, quick acquired the sense of "moving, shifting" and also "fast, swift." The first gives us *quicksand.* The latter is the dominant sense of the word today. The sense of quick meaning "mentally agile" appears around 1450, although there is a single use of *cwices modes*, or "quick mind," in surviving Old English texts.

Ignoramus

Fool, idiot.

Commonly applied now as a pejorative term, *ignoramus* derives from the plural Latin for "we don't know." Though it has negative connotations today, it used to be a simple descriptive term. Until the 17th century, it was used in British courts when juries could not decide a case due to lack of evidence. The 1615 George Ruggle play *Ignoramus,* a farce about a clueless attorney, gave the term its current pejorative meaning. None of Ruggle's other plays survived, but he left his mark on the English language.

Extraterrestrial

Not from this earth; alien life.

Extraterrestrial comes from the Latin words for "outside" and "Earth." It can be either a noun ("an extraterrestrial") or an adjective ("of extraterrestrial origin"). H. G. Wells may have been one of the first to use this word as an adjective, but credit for popularizing its use to refer to beings from another planet goes to L. Sprague de Camp. De Camp used both "extraterrestrial" and its abbreviation, "E.T.," as a noun in the same 1939 *Astounding Science Fiction* article.

Tidy

Neat, organized, clean.

....

The history of the word *tidy* is actually anything but. Its original meaning was "timely, opportune," used particularly in regard to seasonal crops. It comes from the Old English *tid*, a versatile little word that meant "time," "a measure of time" (anything from one hour to many years), or "season." It was in the middle of the 14th century, during the period when Middle English was spoken, that tidy appeared as an adjective meaning "timely."

The Middle English definition could also mean "in good condition, healthy, plump." Originally reserved for crops and livestock, this meaning eventually gained currency as a descriptor for people. From there, tidy expanded to mean "admirable, possessing desirable qualities."

Today's principle meaning ("orderly, clean") dates to at least the beginning of the 18th century, when the word was included in a 1706 dictionary with the definition "handy, neat, clean." A century later, thanks to a linguistic process called *functional shift* —by which a word changes part of speech without any changes to its form—speakers of English gained the option of using tidy as a verb, often paired with *up*.

Hag

A pejorative term for an old, ugly woman.

Hag originally existed in Old English as *hægtesse* and referred to a witch, a fury, or an evil female spirit. Sometime during the Middle English period, it was clipped to *hagge*, getting us closer to the word as we know it today. From its earliest days, hag has had the meaning of "an evil spirit, a female demon." The word was used to refer to the furies and harpies of classical mythology, as well as various female spirits of the Germanic mythos. The word was also used to refer to female spirits believed to visit men at night and it survives in this sense in *night-hag*, the name for the phenomenon of imagined paralysis and hallucination that occurs in some people as they fall asleep.

Hag has also been used as a synonym for witch, or for a woman who is otherwise associated with the devil. It can be applied to any feminine personification of evil or vice. And, of course, it can simply name an ugly, old woman—but there's almost always the connotation of evil or malice.

Credenza

A sideboard, especially one from which food is served.

....

The Latin word *credibilis,* meaning "trustworthy," and the associated verb *credere* ("to trust, rely on, believe") act as the roots of many of our own terms having to do with trustworthiness and believability. *Credibility, credulity,* and *credential* all have to do with believability and trustworthiness, or lack thereof. *Credit* pertains to financial trustworthiness. *Incredible* refers to something that can scarcely be believed.

Believe it or not, *credenza* is from the same root. The modern English word was borrowed from the Italian in the late 19th century, but there was an earlier sense of *credence,* dating to the 16th century, that denoted the piece of furniture. The name comes from the practice of laying out a noble's food on a sideboard so that it could be tasted by a servant to ensure it wasn't poisoned; food on the sideboard, or credenza, could be trusted because it had already been tasted.

INCREDIBLY CREDIBLE

....

A *creed* is a statement of belief. A *miscreant,* before the word came to mean any old villain or reprobate, was originally a heretic, one who believed in false creeds.

MAY 14

Peloton

The main cluster of bicycle riders in a race.

Many people were recently introduced to the word *peloton* through the company of the same name. Peloton Interactive, Inc., sells exercise equipment such as bikes and treadmills, as well as offering streaming exercise classes. Founded in 2012, it surged in popularity during the COVID-19 pandemic. The word, however, is not a brand name. It refers to a pack of riders in a bicycle race. The word derives from the French *peloton,* which can mean a ball, a pack of people, or a group of soldiers; our words *platoon* and *pellet* are related.

MAY 15

Ramshackle

Something that is falling down or crumbling.

Ramshackle sounds a bit like *ransack*, and that isn't a coincidence. It derives from an older form of the word, *ransackled* ("plundered"). A building that had been ransackled might look ramshackle. The modern word can be used for both physical structures (a ramshackle house) or metaphorical ones (a ramshackle plan). Ramshackle dates back to about the 1820s, while ransackled appeared a few centuries before that.

Slogan

A short, memorable phrase used to draw attention to a brand, product, advertisement, or person, or to express the goal or purpose of an organization.

Now the banal realm of advertising companies and political parties, the word *slogan* originally referred to the Gaelic battle cry *sluagh-ghairm* (*sluagh* meaning "army" + *ghairm* meaning "cry"), which invoked the name of the warriors' clan leader as they marched into the fray. In that context, it began appearing in the 1500s. From the original Gaelic it transitioned to *slogorn*, and probably began being used in English in the early 1700s. Historically, slogans were serious business; they could even act as passwords in battle. Today, slogans aren't life or death, but influencers and advertisers would surely attest to their importance. Some of the most memorable corporate slogans in recent years include Nike's "Just do it," Verizon's "Can you hear me now?" and Wendy's "Where's the beef?"

A WHOLE SLEW

From *sluagh*, meaning army or group, we likely also get the noun *slew,* meaning a large number of something. An advertising company might be asked to generate a slew of slogans for its client.

Ovation

Enthusiastic public acclaim, especially in the form of sustained applause.

Most likely, you're familiar with the kind of *ovation* that follows a particularly breathtaking concert, play, or other performance, especially in the phrase *standing ovation*. But the word has a usage quite apart from the concert hall and sports arena. The word originated in classical Latin, and in the world of ancient Rome it had a rather specific application. Upon victorious return 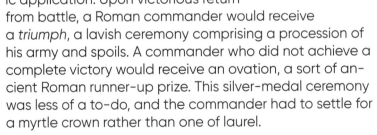 from battle, a Roman commander would receive a *triumph*, a lavish ceremony comprising a procession of his army and spoils. A commander who did not achieve a complete victory would receive an ovation, a sort of ancient Roman runner-up prize. This silver-medal ceremony was less of a to-do, and the commander had to settle for a myrtle crown rather than one of laurel.

Used in its literal sense to describe aspects of ancient Roman civilization, the word ovation first showed up in English texts in the 1500s. Over the next few centuries, the word underwent semantic broadening. By the early 1800s, application of the word had been stretched further, giving us the meaning we are familiar with today.

Rascal

A villain; someone who causes mischief.

The word *rascal* popped up in the 14th century in its Middle English form *rascaile*. In that context it referred less to behavior than to class: a rascal was a person from the masses. The word derived from an Anglo-French word *rascaille* that meant rabble. By the 1600s, however, the word meant what it means today: a dishonest or unprin-cipled person. At that time the word could be used as a noun and an adjective. Today it is used solely as a noun, with the adjective form being "rascally," as in Elmer Fudd's "Rascally Rabbit." The word today can also be used to describe a person or animal who isn't necessarily malicious but does cause trouble.

From rascal we also get the more elaborate *rapscallion*, which appeared in the mid-1600s.

RASCALLY RAPSCALLIONS

Between 1922 and 1944, a series of short films showing a group of mischievous children was marketed under the name *Our Gang*. Later, when the shorts were reis-sued and syndicated to television, *Our Gang* couldn't be used for trademark reasons. They were branded *The Little Rascals* instead.

Tawdry

Cheap and gaudy.

....

The word dates to the 17th century, when it was also a noun meaning "cheap, showy finery." Only the adjective is used much today. *Tawdry* comes to us from *tawdry lace*, an alteration of *St. Audrey's lace,* a silk neckerchief popular with women in the 16th and 17th centuries. The term *tawdry lace* is about a century older than the adjective, appearing in the mid-sixteenth century.

The name comes from the story of Ethelreda, also known as Audrey, an ancient Anglo-Saxon princess who took a vow of perpetual virginity and somehow sustained it through two marriages before taking holy orders. After Audrey's canonization, it became fashionable for medieval English women to wear lacy silk scarves around their necks in tribute to her. Cheap and gaudy versions—of the sort you'd find at any tourist trap today—were sold to the country women at the annual St. Audrey fair at Ely, and after a time such inferior finery gained inextricable association with the chaste saint. This association led to the term *St. Audrey's lace*, which eventually contracted to *tawdry lace.* By the late 17th century, the word tawdry had gained stand-alone status.

Prairie

An area of grassland.

....

The word *prairie* comes ultimately from the Latin *prartum*, meaning a kind of meadow, and traveled to English via the French word *praerie*. While the word first appeared circa 1680, it wasn't frequently used until the days of  exploration of North America. Prairies, and the wide expanses of the Great Plains, became part of the mythology of the United States, with any number of American poets and novelists using them as a topic. William Cullen Bryant (1794–1878) wrote in "The Prairies" that:

These are the gardens of the Desert, these
The unshorn fields, boundless and beautiful,
For which the speech of England has no name—
The Prairies.

Even as prairie land was developed and built up, the concept of the prairie and nostalgia for the days of settlement remained a popular topic. Willa Cather was celebrated for her Prairie trilogy (published 1913–1918), while Laura Ingalls Wilder's popular book, *Little House on the Prairie*, published in 1935, related events that took place in 1874–1875.

Acronym

A word formed by the initial letters of a series of other words.

What do *laser, radar,* and *scuba* have in common? They're all examples of *acronyms,* a rich source of new words coming into the English language. Acronyms (from the Greek *acro-,* meaning "topmost," and *-onym,* "name") combine the initial letters of a series of words to form a new word: *Laser* is **L**ight **A**mplification by **S**timulated **E**mission of **R**adiation; *radar* is **RA**dio **D**etecting **A**nd **R**anging; scuba is **S**elf-**C**ontained **U**nderwater **B**reathing **A**pparatus. The simple programming language BASIC (**B**eginner's **A**ll-purpose **S**ymbolic **I**nstruction **C**ode) is an acronym as well.

World War II produced an alphabet soup of acronyms. Women combatants became *WACs* (**W**omen's **A**rmy **C**orps) and *WAVES* (**W**omen **A**ccepted for **V**olunteer **E**mergency **S**ervice), a branch of the Navy. *Gestapo* (**GE**heime **STA**atsPOlizei, or "Secret State Police") entered English through German, along with *flak* (**FL**ieger**A**bwehr**K**anone, or "aircraft defense gun").

INITIALLY SPEAKING

Similar to acronyms are *initialisms,* which are pronounced not as words but as a series of letters (e.g., FBI, IRS, ASAP).

Calico

A cotton cloth with a pattern printed on it; an animal with a pattern of spots or patches.

Although in America, we usually think of the word *calico* as describing a printed cloth or a patterned cat, the word was first used in the 16th century to describe any cloth that came from Calicut, India. The term was used in England (then referring to plain cotton fabric) as far back as 1578. In the late 1700s and 1800s, when people in the United States began importing that fabric with printed patterns, the word came to describe the pattern as well.

Levity

The quality of being lighthearted; flippancy.

When something *levitates,* it rises up. *Levitation, levitate,* and *levity* are all related words that have to do with lightness, whether literal or figurative. They come via the French from the Latin *levitas,* meaning lightness. When the word levity originated in the 16th century, it referred to physical lightness; it was believed at the time that there was a force—levity—that acted in opposition to gravity, causing some objects to rise. Today, we use the term figuratively, to refer to frivolity.

Terrific

Wonderful, great, stupendous.

....

In contemporary parlance, the adjective *terrific* is typically used in an emphatic, complimentary manner. But terrific meant something quite different historically. The root *terr-*, found in other familiar English words like *terror* and *terrible*, ultimately comes from the Latin verb *terrere,* meaning "to frighten." Terrific began its career as a word describing something frightening or dreadful. The first writer known to use it was John Milton in the 1674 edition of *Paradise Lost.* Milton uses it in the sense of "frightening" as he describes the animals God has created:

The Serpent suttl'st Beast of all the field,
Of huge extent somtimes, with brazen Eyes
And hairie Main terrific, though to thee
Not noxious, but obedient at thy call.

How did this word come to denote something stupendous? Well, terrific, like a host of other adjectives— horrible, terrible, and awful, for instance—semantically broadened over time to denote anything excessive or severe. The *Oxford English Dictionary* dates this decidedly less frightening sense to the early 19th century. From there, it arrived at its current commendatory connotation.

Villain

An evil person.

Today, we think of the *villain* in opposition to the hero. If you used this word in feudal England, though, you would have been referring to a poor but honest person who worked as a serf on a noble's estate. The name comes from the Latin *villanus* ("farm servant"), which indicated simply that the person worked at a *villa*, or Roman country house. Over time, high class began to be associated with politeness and goodness, and so the word evolved to mean a person who wasn't a chivalrous knight—that is, someone capable of base acts.

Rookie

Someone new to a task or skill, a novice.

While the origin of *rookie* is somewhat obscure, it can potentially be traced to both *rook* and *recruit*. A large annoying black bird found in rural medieval England was known as a rook. When young farmers went to the local fairs and were taken by the swindlers there, they compared the thieves to the rooks; ultimately, those conned in the swindle became known as rookies. The word came to be used in modern language to describe anyone young, naïve, or new at something.

Pilgrim

A traveler, especially someone who travels to a religious site.

The word *pilgrim* first appeared in English circa 1200. It came from the French words *pelerin* and *peregrin,* meaning stranger or foreigner, which in turn came from the Latin *peregrinus.* The concept of the pilgrimage appeared much earlier, and crosses religious boundaries. In ancient Greece, pilgrims traveled to seek counsel from oracles. Early Christian church father Saint Jerome (c. 342–420) encouraged pilgrimages to Christian sites, while the Hajj, the pilgrimage to Mecca that Muslims undertake at least once in their lifetime, is one of the five pillars of Islam.

Some of the most famous fictional pilgrims include the travelers on the road to the shrine of Thomas Becket who told their stories in Geoffrey Chaucer's *The Canterbury Tales.* Chaucer's work was written between 1387 and 1400, and describes how every Spring, "longen folk to goon on pilgrimages."

When capitalized, the term refers to the English settlers who came to Plymouth, Massachusetts, aboard the *Mayflower* in 1620. While William Bradford, a member of the settlement, used the term in passing in his recounting of the settlement to refer to his compatriots, the usage didn't pick up steam until more than 150 years later.

MAY 28

Panacea

A cure-all or all-purpose medicine.

....

In Greek mythology, the goddess *Panakeia* was the daughter of Asclepius, the god of medicine, and his wife Epione, which meant "soothing." Panakeia had a number of brothers and sisters who each represented some facet of healing, and she herself was the goddess of universal health. Her name came from the Greek words *pan* ("all") and *akos* ("remedy"). From its Greek roots the word made its way to the Latin *panacea,* and from there to English. Various herbs or combinations of herbs have been dubbed *panaceas.* The Valerian plant *(Valeriana officinalis)* for example, once had the common name *all-heal.* Today, the term *panacea* is almost always used skeptically and a little derisively.

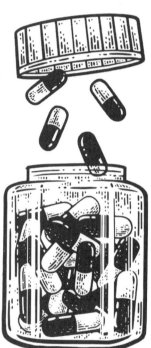

A VERY TIDY DEITY

....

One of Panakeia's sisters was *Hygieia,* the goddess of cleanliness and sanitation. From her name we get the word *hygiene.*

MAY 29

Obmutescence

The process of becoming silent; the act of remaining silent.

....

In the middle of the word *obmutescence,* you can pick out the word *mute.* That's no accident. In Latin, *ob-* means "towards" and *mutus* means "mute." From these roots developed the Latin verb *obmutescere,* to become mute (or, literally, to move towards muteness). In the 17th century, the word transitioned to English. While the word can refer to becoming unable to speak, it can also carry a connotation of deliberately choosing not to speak.

MAY 30

Sodality

A close group; companionship.

....

Fraternities, tight-knit book clubs, and bowling leagues are all examples of *sodalities:* groups of people bound together into an association. The word first appears in English circa 1600, coming from the French *sodalité* and before that from the Latin *sodalis,* a word meaning "companion." The word refers to both the group itself and the sense of community found there: that is, you might join a sodality in search of sodality. While the word can be used to refer to any organized group, you may see it specifically used for organizations of Roman Catholic laypeople that form to do charitable works or to share devotional practices.

Kibosh

Something that stops or halts something else.

Used almost exclusively in the phrase "put the *kibosh* on," the word has a very mysterious etymology. One early usage was by Charles Dickens in 1836 in *Sketches by Boz*, although he uses an alternate spelling. Describing a public argument between some women, he has a bystander declare, "[P]ut the kye-bosk on her, Mary!" Some contemporaneous newspapers also use the term, mostly spelling it "kibosh." Some of these usages predate Dickens by a few years, so it seems to have been a known London slang term at the time.

Where it originated, though, no one really knows. Various people have suggested that it comes from *kurbash* (a whip; the word comes from Turkish), an Irish phrase *caidhp bháis* that means death cap, or the French word *caboche* (meaning head). For now, it remains a mystery.

Macaroni

A type of pasta shaped like small tubes. Obsolete: a dandy or fop.

....

The Italian words *maccaroni* (plural) and *maccarone* (singular) date back to the late 16th century and referred to a food made from flour, cheese, and butter. From there, we get both the English word *macaroni* for the pasta and the French word *macaron,* which became the English word *macaroon,* for the sweet treat.

Though macaroni and cheese is a staple dish of childhood now, its continental origins once gave it a glamorous cachet in Britain. During that time, the word also referred to a set of well-traveled, aristocratic young gentlemen from Britain who were teased for being slavish followers of the latest trends from Italy and France. There may even have been a Macaroni Club in Britain in the 1760s whose members borrowed their name from the food, and who wore elaborate "macaroni wigs." Today, that sense of the word survives for us mainly in the song "Yankee Doodle Dandy," referring to a man who thinks he's reached the height of fashion because he's stuck a feather in his cap.

Onion

The herb *Allium cepa*, or its bulb.

A close relative of a number of pungent herbs like garlic and leeks, the common onion was described by Carl Linnaeus in 1753. *Allium cepa* refers to the domesticated variety, but there are a number of wild species in the larger Allium family. Onions have been cultivated for food for at least 7,000 years, with domestication probably occurring in Asia. They were a popular food in ancient Rome, along with garlic.

The word *onion* first appears in the 14th century in Middle English, related to the French *oignon*, and deriving ultimately from the Latin *unio,* meaning "one." How that Latin word got linked to the vegetable is a bit unclear, but one theory holds that because the onion was a single bulb, rather than a cluster of bulbs like garlic, it was associated with unity.

The Latin word for onion was *cepa*, which shows up in the common onion's scientific name. The word *allium* was the Latin term for garlic (known scientifically as *Allium sativum).*

JUNE 3

Sanguine

Hopeful, optimistic.

....

Here's a weird one. The word derives from the Middle English word *sanguine,* which means blood. In this case, "blood" is a happy word, meaning cheerful confidence and optimism. In those days, people thought the body was made up of four humors, or bodily fluids. If your predominant humor was blood, you'd have a ruddy face and cheerful personality. The similar-looking word, *sanguinary,* comes from a related Latin root but is not so positive. It actually means bloodthirsty.

JUNE 4

Marshmallow

A sweet treat made of gelatin and sugar.

....

The Proto-Indo-European root *mori* means "body of water, lake, or sea." *Marsh* comes to us by way of *mori,* and *mallow* is likely from the Latin word *malva* ("to soften"). Through translations and a good measure of miscommunication, you get *marsh mallow,* the name for "a plant that grows in marshes." The root of the marsh mallow yields a thick, gluey sap that was first used for medicinal purposes; in the late 19th century, a confection was created from it. These days, the *marshmallows* you put in your cocoa are mostly sugar and gelatin, with no sap in sight.

Cereal

A plant that produces grain; the grain it produces; a non-perishable food made from grain.

What's the tie between your daily bowl of Cheerios and Roman mythology? The word *cereal* comes from the name of the Roman goddess *Ceres*. Modeled after the Greek goddess Demeter, Ceres was the goddess of both agriculture and fertility. Some of her symbols, such as wheat sheaves, were based on grain crops. In April, the ancient Romans held a weeklong festival, called *Cerealia,* to honor her. Despite the word's ancient roots, it didn't appear in English until early in the 19th century, appearing first as an adjective and then as a noun about a decade later.

A GRAIN OF TRUTH

Cold prepared breakfast cereals started appearing in the United States with the 1836 introduction of one named Granula. Several cereals were invented in Battle Creek, Michigan, in the late 1800s. The Kellogg brothers got their start in a sanitorium for healthy living and developed Corn Flakes in that capacity. A patient of theirs, Charles Post, recuperated there and then, based on the diet he remembered, went on to develop Grape-nuts.

Pink

As an adjective, a hue of red. As a verb, to cut a patterned edge or to pierce. As a noun, a flower in the genus *Dianthus*.

. . . .

The word *pink* has a number of diverse usages with hazy roots. Pink first shows up as a verb as early as 1200. In that context, it meant to wound someone by using a pointed weapon. In the centuries that followed, the word broadened to reflect the idea of putting holes in things other than flesh, especially to create a decorative pattern in cloth. That usage evolved over time to leave us today with *pinking shears*, which cut the edges of fabric with a sawtooth pattern.

In the late 16th century, flowers from the genus *Dianthus* begin to be called *pinks*. This might derive from a Dutch word meaning "small," but accounts vary. This shortly led to a figurative meaning: the pink of something was the best example of something. In the way we might say figuratively that a person is "in the flower of youth," we could also describe someone as being "in the pink of fashion." It wasn't until the first half of the 18th century that the word began to be used to describe the color of many flowers in the *Dianthus* genus.

JUNE 7

Riposte

In fencing, a quick counterattack; a quick verbal retort.

A *riposte* is a response of sorts, and ultimately comes from the Latin verb *responder.* From Latin, the word transitioned to the Italian verb *risposta,* and then to the French *riposte,* which was used in the context of fencing to describe a counterattack made after a fencer fended off a parry. In the early 1700s, the word leapt from French to English fencing. By the mid-1800s, the word was being used in English to describe a sharp, witty, verbal comeback.

JUNE 8

Aphotic

Used to describe the zone in deep bodies of water where plants cannot photosynthesize because there is too little sunlight.

The Greek prefix *a-* signifies something negative. The Greek word for light is *phos.* Put them together—in English, this happened in about 1894—and you describe a place without light.

The *aphotic* zone, which starts at depths of around 660 feet, is the deepest and darkest part of the ocean. While photosynthesis cannot take place there, the aphotic zone is not devoid of life. Phytoplankton abound, and various bioluminescent animals like the anglerfish and the vampire squid live there as well.

Providence

Frugality or prudence with resources; divine guidance. When capitalized, used to refer to God.

Providence obviously sounds similar to *provide,* and both words ultimately originate with the Latin *providentia,* meaning foresight. Providentia was personified as a virtue who appeared on a number of Roman coins.

Today, providence can refer to your own efforts to prepare for the future—that is, to provide for your future self—so you might say, "He was able to pay unexpected expenses because of his providence in putting away money each month." Providence can also refer, however, to divine providence. When the word came to the English in the late 14th century via the Old French *providence,* it carried that connotation of divine guidance and intervention. Around 1600, the word Providence also began to be a sort of direct referent for God.

A CAPITAL FACT

The capital of Rhode Island, Providence, was established in 1636 by Roger Williams, who had been exiled by the Massachusetts Bay Colony.

JUNE 10

Labefaction

The act of weakening or overthrowing order.

....

This obscure word comes to us from the Latin *labare*, meaning "to totter" and *facere* "to make." The noun dates back to about 1775, although several verb forms, now effectively defunct, existed before that. In the 1600s, to *labefy* something was to weaken it, and the verb *labefact* appeared even before that.

JUNE 11

Metage

An official measurement of weight; the payment you make for that measurement.

....

To *mete* is to give out something (as in, "to mete out punishment"), but it was once used to describe the process of measuring something. The verb came from the Old English *metan,* which in turn came from a Proto-Germanic word, both of which meant "to measure." You might measure something before giving it out or distributing it. The noun *metage* likewise refers to measurement; though little used now, it referred to the weighing of goods, especially coal, or the fee you paid to have goods weighed.

Yard

A unit of measurement equal to three feet; or, the grounds surrounding a house.

The word *yard* names both a unit of measurement and the land around your house, but there is a different origin for each meaning. Although both come from Old English, they derive from different roots.

Yard as a unit of measure comes from the Old English *gyrd*, which originally meant "stick, twig." It came to mean a "staff or pole" used for various purposes. The Anglo-Saxons also used *gyrd* to refer to a unit of measure, but one considerably longer than our modern 36 inches. An Anglo-Saxon *gyrd* was roughly 16.5 feet. In the 14th century, 13.5 feet were lopped off the length of a yard (accounts vary as to why), and King Edward III standardized the unit of measure at a length of three feet.

The grassy area around your house, on the other hand, comes from the Old English *geard,* meaning "an enclosure, a dwelling place"—specifically the grounds around a building that were not used for cultivation, but for other work or for living. So we may measure our yards in yards, but despite looking and sounding the same, these are very different words.

Rusticate

To go live in the country for a while; to cause to live in the country; especially in Britain, to suspend or expel a student from school and send them home.

The Latin word *rusticus* ("from the country") gave us the adjective *rustic*. The related verb *rusticatus* gave us *rusticate,* which shows up in English in the mid-1600s. A city dweller might rusticate in the country to regain health, to let a scandal die down, or to live more simply and inexpensively. In the 18th century, the word took on a specific meaning for students, especially those who lived in boarding schools: if they were suspended for a time or outright expelled and sent away from school, they were said to be rusticated.

The term *rusticate* also has a very specific meaning in architecture, where it refers to a masonry technique. Rusticated facades are ones where the masonry blocks have purposefully rough textures or surfaces.

Oobleck

A viscous substance that acts as a liquid at rest but turns solid under pressure.

A lot of school-aged children have done the simple experiment of creating slime, aka *oobleck,* from kitchen ingredients like cornstarch, water, shampoo, and food coloring. Oobleck is a non-Newtonian fluid. The viscosity of non-Newtonian fluids changes depending on the forces of pressure applied. Applying pressure to the slime increases its viscosity, or thickness. When you handle the slime gently, the starch molecules can move around, suspended in the water. This makes a slow-flowing liquid. But when you press down suddenly on the slime, the starch molecules lock together, making the slime feel more solid.

The word comes from that creative master of wordplay Theodore Geisel, aka Dr. Seuss, who published *Bartholomew and the Oobleck* in 1949. Seuss was a prolific creator of nonsense words like *snergelly, schloppity schlop,* and *sneetch,* and some of his words made it into the general vernacular. His neologism *nerd,* used to describe a quirky zoo animal, was picked up and adapted. He also famously coined the term *grinch.*

JUNE 15

Cantankerous

Cranky, contrary, difficult.

....

Cantankerous shows up in English in the 18th century, with somewhat mysterious origins. It may derive from a Middle English word, *contakour,* from the 1300s. *Contakour* was a noun used for a difficult person. Another Middle English word, *contack,* meant animosity, and cantankerous might have evolved as its adjective form. The word also may have been shaped in usage by its similarity to the word *rancorous.* We simply don't know, but that uncertainty might produce a cantankerous debate!

JUNE 16

Pandiculation

A large stretch of the body, especially when drowsy or upon waking.

....

If you've ever instinctively stretched your arms out and yawned as you've woken up, you've engaged in pandiculation. Though the word isn't used frequently, it has survived from its introduction to English in the 1610s. It comes from a Latin word, *pandiculari,* that means "to stretch oneself," which in turn came from an earlier Latin word, *pandere,* "to stretch or spread." A more common word from the same root is *expand:* during pandiculation, you expand your limbs to take up more space.

Caramel

A type of candy made from sugar; the color of the candy.

....

Caramel shows up in English in the early 18th century. A number of Romance languages have similar terms: in French, *caramel;* in Spanish, *caramelo;* in Portuguese, *caramelo.* They all ultimately come from a Latin term, but there's some uncertainty as to that term. Some sources trace it to the late Latin *calamellus,* meaning a reed, but others attribute it to medieval Latin *cannamellis* (*cana,* "cane," + *mel,* "honey.") When the word first showed up in English, it referred to burnt sugar, but later came to refer to the candy we know by that name, and by the early 1900s to the color of that candy.

Fungible

As an adjective, interchangeable, capable of being substituted, often used in reference to money or commodities; adaptable; as a noun, something that is fungible.

....

The word *fungible* showed up in English in 1765 as a noun, and about fifty years later as an adjective. In ancient Roman law, *res fungibilis* was a legal term that meant "replaceable things," and a related Latin verb, *fungi,* meant "to perform." (*Fungi* in Latin is related to the English word *function,* not the plural of the biological classification *fungus.*) The Medieval Latin *fungibilis* in turn became the English fungible.

Bespoke

Made to order.

Something that is *bespoke* is custom-made, designed to fit a particular person; a formal gown, expensive suit, or pair of fancy shoes might be bespoke instead of ready-made. The word appeared in English, using that sense, in the mid-1700s. It's the adjective form of a verb that dates back to around 1580, *bespeak*. One meaning of "to bespeak" is to order something in advance; thus, something ordered in advance can be described as bespoke.

Bespeak, in turn, comes from the Old English *besprecan,* to speak about—or to complain. That meaning of bespeak has fallen by the wayside, although the word still has several usages. To bespeak is to arrange something beforehand, but also can mean to request something or to signify something. In that usage, someone's bespoke clothing might bespeak, or indicate, their wealth.

JUNE 20

Copypasta

A block of text spread widely on the Internet.

....

In 2015, social media posts containing the screenplay for the film *Bee Movie* proliferated across the Internet. This was a famous example of *copypasta*, a word then about a decade old. Created by mashing together the words copy, paste, and pasta, the Internet slang term first showed up in 2006 to refer to any block of text that users pick up from one forum and disseminate to another, sometimes to be annoying. The popular site Reddit has a subforum dedicated to notable examples of copypasta.

JUNE 21

Hazard

As a noun, something that may cause problems; a risk; a danger; as a verb, to take a risk, to venture.

....

For us today, the terms *hazardous materials* and *hazardous waste* evoke high stakes and extreme, even life-threatening danger. But the noun *hazard* comes to us from a game. Back around 1300, hazard was a dice game that relied on chance; the British borrowed the game and the word from the French, who called it *hasard* or *hasart*. The French may have gotten the name for their game from the Arabic word for dice, *az-zahr*. The verb form of *hazard*, meaning to take a chance, showed up in the 1500s.

Nefandous

Unspeakably horrible and shocking.

Nefandous sounds quite similar to *nefarious* and has much the same meaning: a *nefandous* act is a shockingly heinous one. From the Latin negative *ne-* and the Latin *fandus*, "to be spoken," the word literally translates to "unspeakable." The term dates to about 1630 and was used for offensive acts, and especially those that might offend one's sense of piety. It's considered archaic nowadays, though horror writer H.P. Lovecraft used it as recently as 1931, writing in his novella "On the Mountains of Madness:" "It had only horror, because I knew unerringly the monstrous, nefandous analogy that had suggested it."

Nefarious, which has such a similar sound and usage, comes from a different though related Latin root. *Nefas* was the Latin noun meaning crime, a combination of the negative *ne-* and *fas*, the word for divine law. It also appeared around 1600, which raises a question about how many nefandous, nefarious acts were happening at the time to need multiple words to describe them!

Lachrymose

Weepy, prone to cause crying.

Lacrima, the Latin word for tear, serves as the root for a number of words related to the physical act of crying and the sad emotions that might provoke tears. Your tear ducts are called your *lachrymal* glands. *Lachrymation* is the medical term that refers to crying or to the excessive secretion of tears. And *lachrymose* is an adjective meaning "weeping" or "prone to cause crying"; the word is used to describe sad and perhaps melodramatic things. The word can describe both something that makes you weepy, like a tearjerker of a movie, and a person experiencing those emotions. That is, watching a lachrymose drama might make you lachrymose.

Lachrymal has a longer history in the English language, dating back to the 1400s, while lachrymose appears later, in the early 1700s. Be aware that lachrymal and lachryma-tion both have acceptable variant spellings: lacrimal and lacrimation, respectively. Lachrymose, however, is never spelled *lacrimose.*

JUNE 24

Argot

Jargon; in-group language.

....

Today, *argot* refers to any in-group lingo; trade groups, sports teams, professors, and theater companies might all use the argot of their field. The English word was borrowed in the early 19th century from the French word *argot,* where it originated as a term referring to cant used by thieves and mendicants. The process by which the word entered French, however, is fairly opaque—as opaque, perhaps, as any group's argot is to outsiders.

JUNE 25

Caravan

As a noun, a procession of vehicles or pack animals; a group traveling together. As a verb, to travel in such a group.

....

The noun entered English in the late 16th century; it took about three centuries for the verb form to follow. The word ultimately derives from the Persian word *kārvān*, though sources are split on whether it traveled to English from the Middle French *caravane* and the Old French *carvane* that preceded it, the Italian *caravana,* or the Medieval Latin *caravana.* In the late 17th century, the word also came to apply to a large covered carriage or wagon, and in England today a caravan is basically equivalent to an RV in the United States.

Jumbo

Large, oversized.

Something huge can be called *elephantine*, so perhaps it's appropriate that a synonym for huge, *jumbo*, came from an actual elephant. In the early 1880s, famed circus maven P. T. Barnum bought an elephant that he dubbed Jumbo. In the course of advertising, "jumbo" became the word to describe anything that, like the famous elephant, was huge.

Jumbo was an African elephant that Barnum bought from a British zoo, and he proved to be a popular attraction in the United States. He weighed more than six metric tons and stood more than ten feet tall—though Barnum fudged the elephant's dimensions a bit, advertising him as more than thirteen feet tall.

Jumbo died in a train accident in 1885, but he left his stamp on American culture. Because Barnum was a benefactor to Tufts University, Jumbo the elephant became their official mascot, and his stuffed hide stood in P.T. Barnum Hall there until a fire ripped through the building decades later. In the Disney movie *Dumbo* (released in 1941), the titular character's official name is Jumbo Jr.

Sarcasm

A form of irony that uses witty humor to express contempt.

The word *sarcasm* comes from the Greek *sarkazein,* meaning "to tear flesh," or later, "to bite the lips in anger" or "to speak bitterly." Sarcasm is a form of dry humor that relies on understatement rather than revealing emotion. It mocks as it amuses. It means to hurt, and it quite often succeeds.

The technique is very old, dating back even to biblical times. Although one might not expect to find sarcasm in the Bible, it's there. In the *Book of Exodus,* the Israelites, impatient with their trek through the wilderness and the lack of food, reproach Moses sarcastically: "Because there were no graves in Egypt, hast thou taken us away to die in the wilderness?" (14:11 KJV).

Sarcasm is often considered a low form of humor, because often its form is simple. It doesn't take much wit for a basketball player to taunt an opponent who just missed the net with "Nice shot!" However, sarcasm can also be more sophisticated. Shakespeare was a master of the form, using harsh sarcasm as when, in *Julius Caesar,* Mark Antony repeatedly refers to Brutus as "an honorable man."

Barbecue

As a verb, to cook food, especially meat, either by a method that involves smoking it over low heat, or by a method that involves placing it on a rack or spit over a heat source; as a noun, the food cooked by that method, the fireplace or pit used to barbecue food, or the social event where barbecued food is eaten.

Barbecue has been around for centuries. The word appeared in English as a verb in the late 17th century, and as a noun about forty years later. The word comes from the Spanish *barbacoa,* which came from the Taino *barbakoa,* referring to the wooden apparatus used in the West Indies to cook meat over a fire. The word showed up in several sources in the 1600s, and by the mid-1700s the word was established well enough that Samuel Johnson included it in his 1756 dictionary in both noun and verb forms, writing: "To Barbecue—a term for dressing a whole hog" and "Barbecue—a hog dressed whole."

BBQ FYI

In the United States, we abbreviate barbeque to BBQ, a shortening that began to appear circa 1950. The Australians call it barbie.

Debauch

To corrupt, to seduce; an occasion of debauchery.

....

Debauch can be used as both a verb and a noun. Someone tempting younger, innocent people to an orgy, for example, would be debauching them by inviting them to a debauch. One prone to debauchery is a *debauchee*.

In English, both the verb and noun forms of debauch date back to about 1600, and were taken from the French word *débaucher*, which in turn comes from the Old French *desbaucher*. While the earlier twists and turns of the word's etymology are a bit hazier, "bauch" may ultimately derive from a German word for "beam."

While the French words were related to leading someone astray, or distracting them from a task they should be doing, they didn't necessarily imply sexual corruption. The current French verb *débaucher* still has a range of meanings. While it can mean "to corrupt, especially sexually," it can also carry more innocent connotations, relating to distracting someone from work or even letting someone go from a job because of lack of work. In English, however, the overtone of sexual corruption has prevailed.

Nostalgia

A state in which someone remembers past events or periods with a mixture of both happiness and melancholy. Previously, homesickness.

The word *nostalgia* was reportedly created by a Swiss physician, Johannes Hofer (1669–1752), in his 1688 dissertation. He used New Latin to create the term from the Greek *nostos* ("homecoming") and *algia* ("distress"). To Hofer and many after him, nostalgia was a medical problem, a severe homesickness that compromised health. In the centuries that followed, nostalgia showed up in medical manuals in Europe and the United States, especially in reference to soldiers far away from home. Soldiers could be punished or shamed for succumbing to nostalgia, and there could be an "outbreak" in which nostalgia spread through a group of soldiers. In an account shortly after the U.S. Civil War, the U.S. Sanitary Commission reported, "In the first two years of the war, there were reported 2588 cases of nostalgia, and 13 deaths from this cause. These numbers scarcely express the real extent to which nostalgia influenced the sickness and mortality of the army."

Our current sense of the word nostalgia has only existed for a century or so, dating to the early 20th century.

Carceral

Related to imprisonment.

. . . .

Incarceration is imprisonment, and to *incarcerate* someone is to imprison them. These two words, and the related adjective *carceral,* all come from the same Latin root, *carcer* ("prison"). The word showed up in the 1570s in English. In the United States, you'll hear the term *carceral state* used to refer to America's extensive jail and prison systems, as the United States has both the highest number of people in prisons in the world and the highest incarceration rate in the world.

Ombudsman

A person at an organization, institution, or government agency whose role is to act on behalf of customers, patients, and employees in order to resolve issues and complaints.

. . . .

The word *ombudsman* originated in Sweden in the 20th century, and literally translates to "commission man." While any organization might have an ombudsman, they are generally standard at hospitals and rehab facilities, sometimes under the title "Patient Advocate." In the United States, the Older Americans Act required each state to set up a Long-Term Care Ombudsman program. If your loved one is in a nursing home or assisted living facility and receiving substandard care, that program might be a resource.

Focaccia

A type of seasoned flatbread.

....

Borrowed directly from Italian, *focaccia* was first used in English in the 1880s. The Italian, in turn, ultimately derives from the Latin word *focus*, translating to "fireplace" or "hearth."

Focaccia is made from high-gluten flour, oil, water, yeast, and salt, and generally topped with herbs and cheese. In Italy, the region of Liguria is especially known for its focac- cia (it's called *fugassa* in Ligurian), but dif- ferent regions of Italy have different variations. In Northwest Italy, you can even find a sweet variation. The basic recipe may pre- date the Roman Empire and have originated with the an- cient Etruscans.

The word has a number of cognates in the languages of nearby countries. The Provencal region of France offers a flatbread called *fougasse*, *hogaza* is the Spanish word for "loaf," and Portugal has a sweet bread named *fogaça*.

Praxis

Action; the applied practice of a theory; the collection of examples being used for practice.

··

The ancient Greek *praxis* meant "activity" or "action," contrasting with theory. The word traveled from the Greek to the Latin and showed up in the English in the late 16th century. Various fields use the term in related but field-specific ways. In philosophy, for example, the term is used, especially in Marxism, with the idea of acting to effect societal change. Karl Marx himself used the term, writing, "All social life is essentially practical. All the mysteries which lead theory towards mysticism find their rational solution in human praxis and in the comprehension of this praxis."

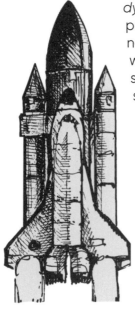

Aristotle used the terms *eupraxia* and *dyspraxia* to refer to good and bad practice. Today, those terms have a narrower medical meaning. Along with *apraxia*, they are used to refer to someone's capacity in terms of motor skills and coordination.

THERE WILL BE A TEST

··

The Praxis exams are a set of teacher certification exams. Some states require that prospective teachers take one or more of these exams. College students in teaching programs may also take these exams at certain milestones.

JULY 5

Frisson

A sudden sensation of excitement; a shiver produced by a thrill.

. . . .

A *frisson* of excitement or fear might cause you to shiver, which is appropriate since the word comes from the French *frisson,* meaning shiver. The French, in turn, came from the Latin words *frictio* and *frigeo,* "to be cold." The French word dates back to the 1100s, and it hopped over to English in 1777, although it didn't see wider use until about a century later.

JULY 6

Decal

An image made to be transferred from paper to another surface; a sticker.

. . . .

In Latin, *calquer* meant "to press" and that sense of pressing something traveled through the Italian *calcare* to the French verb *décalquer*, which referred to the process of pressing a picture on a specially treated paper to a hard surface like glass in order to transfer it. The related French noun for the transferred picture was *décalcomanie*. Décalcomanie became a bit of a trend in Frrance in the middle of the 19th century. When the trend made it across the British Channel a few decades later, the British called those pictures *decalcomania*. Eventually, in the early 20th century, the word was shortened to *decal*.

Android

A robot with a human form.

....

Popularized in the 1950s by science fiction writers, the word that means "automaton resembling a human being" actually goes back to approximately 1730 (from the Greek *andro-*, "human," *eides*, "form"). An English encyclopedia referenced one that was supposedly created by a friar and scholar in the 1200s. In the United States, the term was used in patents in the mid-1800s to refer to small mechanical dolls.

Related terms are *replicant* (from *replica*, or "exact copy") in the 1982 film *Blade Runner* (which was adapted from the novel *Do Androids Dream of Electric Sheep?* by Philip K. Dick), and *mecha* ("mechanical person") used in the film *Artificial Intelligence: A.I.* (2001). And, of course, the Star Wars franchise popularized the shortened term of the word, *droid*.

THERE'S ONE IN YOUR PHONE

....

The Android operating system for smartphones and tablets was revealed in 2007. Google holds the trademark on the "Android" name and logo.

144

Conundrum

A perplexing problem; more narrowly, a word-based riddle.

The word *conundrum* first appeared in print in 1596 and was spelled *quonundrum*, reflecting the then-fashionable academic humor of inventing Latin words to poke fun at current events and situations. The word initially described someone who was overly pedantic or fussy about a seemingly unimportant point.

By 1646, conundrum had evolved to denote any bit of confusing wordplay, especially an insulting one. In the 1700s, it began to refer specifically to a riddle based on a pun or verbal trickery. Some sticklers still hold that it can only mean a riddle involving wordplay, one in which a fanciful question is answered with a play on words—for example, "What cannot be bought, cannot be sold, even if it's made of gold?" (a heart).

By the end of the century, however, it was commonly used in reference to any mind-bending puzzle, especially one without an easy answer—for example, "Which came first, the chicken or the egg?" Despite the continued cry from modern English purists to keep conundrum from acquiring a meaning beyond that of a punny problem, that battle was lost nearly 300 years ago.

Gerrymander

To divide a geographic area into voting districts so that one political party has an unfair advantage in elections; a district produced by the process; the act of gerrymandering.

....

The U.S. Constitution requires that a census be taken every ten years and that state legislatures redraw the districts of the House of Representatives to reflect changes in population. Of course, this creates plenty of opportunity for political mischief, as each political party seeks to redraw the district boundaries to favor its own electoral chances.

One of the early egregious examples of this practice occurred in 1812 in Essex County, Massachusetts. The Massachusetts legislature, dominated by Democratic-Republicans, drew one district so that it snaked around the borders of the county, favoring their party. Elbridge Gerry, who was the Democratic-Republican governor at the time, did not support the redistricting plan but reluctantly signed it into law because of his party's wishes—but as the party's leader, he was given credit for the plan in the popular imagination.

The district's serpentine shape inspired painter and sometime political cartoonist Gilbert Stuart to sketch a head, feet, and wings on the drawing of the district and label it a "salamander." Stuart submitted the cartoon to the *Boston Centinel,* whose editor, Benjamin Russell, captioned it with the name "Gerrymander." Thus a political term was born.

Silhouette

As a noun, either a piece of art that shows a filled-in outline of an object or person, or an object lit in such a way so that you can only see its general shape; as a verb, to silhouette.

Silhouette is an eponym, coming from French minister of finance named Étienne de Silhouette (1709–1767). Why his name was connected is a bit unclear. Silhouettes were a popular way of capturing someone's likeness during his tenure, and it may have been as simple as that. Some sources suggest he either collected silhouettes or created simple ones as a hobby. Another idea is that since he was notoriously cheap, and unpopular for his frugality, his name became slang for cheapness or cheap objects. As likeness-es, silhouettes were inexpensive as compared to traditional portraits. Whatever the case, the word came into use in the mid-18th century. By the middle of the 19th century the meaning had broadened to encompass not only likenesses purposefully created as silhouettes but objects that had the appearance of silhouettes; for example, "We saw the silhouette of an enemy soldier on the ridge." The verb form appeared in the late 19th century.

JULY 11

Obelus

The symbol used for division (÷); a symbol used to indicate a potentially doubtful passage in translated text.

An *obelus* or *obolus* (plural *obeli*) is a symbol, usually a short horizonal line with a dot or multiple dots, that was once used in ancient texts to note that the reader should be skeptical about a particular word or an entire passage.[†] The word entered the language in the 14th century from the late Latin *obelus,* meaning a mark, which borrowed from the comparable Greek *obelus.*

† In typography, the dagger symbol used to indicate that the reader should consult a footnote or endnote is also referred to as an obelus.

JULY 12

Tergiversation

Equivocation, deliberate evasion of a clear answer; abandonment of a previously held principle, stance, or commitment.

The word *tergiversation,* and the related verb *to tergiver-sate,* comes from the Latin word *tergiversatio* ("to display hesitation"). That word breaks down to the roots te*rgum* ("back") and *versare* ("to turn"). It showed up in English around 1560. If you wanted to be fancy, you might accuse an evasive or flip-flopping politician of tergiversation.

Anesthesia

Something that dulls or removes sensation; the loss of sensation.

....

This Latin term was first seen in 1721 and comes from Greek roots. *An-* indicates a negative and *aísthēsis* refers to feeling. Its use in medicine, however, referring to a substance used to muffle or eradicate pain during a surgical procedure, didn't happen until 1846.

Various substances have been used throughout medical history as *anesthetics*. Some Arabic physicians in the 11th century had their patients inhale narcotic drugs from a sponge in order to perform surgery. Japanese doctor Hanaoka Seishū used an herbal formula that acted as a general anesthetic in the early 1800s.

In the United States, several men began to use ether in the 1840s. Surgeon Crawford Long performed an 1842 operation with it, although he didn't publicize his work until the late 1840s. Dentist Horace Wells demonstrated the use of nitrous oxide in 1845, but the dose wasn't given properly and the patient still experienced some pain. In 1846, dentist William Morton held a successful demonstration using ether. News quickly spread, and it was Morton's friend, physician and poet Oliver Wendall Holmes, Sr., who suggested the term anesthesia for the state induced by the new wonder drug.

Dunce

A dolt, a person who is not smart.

....

Dunce has an interesting history: It actually comes from the name of a *smart* person. The word began as an eponym of the thirteenth-century theologian and thinker Jon Duns Scotus. Duns was never considered a dunce himself, but he attracted many followers, and they developed a not-so-bright reputation.

Up until the 16th century, Duns was considered a formidable intellectual figure. His texts on theology, philosophy, and logic were staples in respected English universities. As time went on, however, Duns's ideas became outdated, and adherents of other schools of thought pounced on them as objects of ridicule. Duns's loyalists—the Dunsmen, or Dunses—remained steadfast in their increasingly unpopular beliefs, making them easy academic targets.

Eventually, *Dunse* adopted the connotation of—as the *Oxford English Dictionary* puts it today—a "blockhead incapable of learning or scholarship." Within only a few decades, the word was being applied more broadly. You no longer had to be a stubborn follower of Duns to be a *Dunse*. With this more liberal application came a change in the spelling and the loss of the initial capital letter.

JULY 15

Astrobleme

A blemish on the Earth's crust or surface caused by meteorite impact.

Were it not for the gradual process of erosion, the Earth's face would look a lot more blemished. *Astrobleme* (somewhere there's an irreverent teenager taking liberties with this word) was coined by geophysicist Robert Sinclair Dietz in 1961 to describe terrestrial impact structures. It comes from the Greek roots *astro* ("star") and *bleme* ("wound caused by a missile"). The term impact crater is often used synonymously.

JULY 16

Scurrilous

Vulgar, coarse, or foul-mouthed.

The infamous lexicographer Samuel Johnson defined *scurrilous* as "using such language as only the licence [sic] of a buffoon could warrant." The kind of off-color banter and joking heard in the rowdiest dive bar in town might qualify as scurrilous. So too would any harsh jokes or ridicule whose intent is actually to harm or slander. The word comes from the French *scurrile*, which in turn came from the Latin source word *scurrilis* ("buffoonlike").

Grenade

A small explosive object that is launched or thrown by hand.

Compare the words *pomegranate* and *grenade*. Are the words related? Did someone have a macabre sense of humor? Indeed, the word grenade did evolve out of a French word for the fruit. In fact, grenades were first called pomegranates. The similarities between the many-seeded fruit and the fragmenting bomb were apparently enough to get the point across. If you were to crack open a hand grenade, you would see tiny pieces of shrapnel arrayed inside the casing. The configuration resembles the seeds packed into a pomegranate.

There's an unfortunate irony in this: traditionally, across multiple cultures, the pomegranate has been a symbol of fertility, plenty, harmony, and resurrection—not death-dealing explosions.

A POMEGRANATE A DAY

So what about the fruit's etymological origin? The Old French *pome grenate* comes from the Latin *pomum granatum* ("apple with many seeds"). *Granum* is a particularly rich source word, and has given us *grain*, *grange*, *grainite*, *granule*, *grenadine*, and *kernel*, among many others.

Assassin

Someone who commits murder for political or ideological reasons.

....

Assassin comes from a variously-spelled medieval French and Italian word (*assissini* is a frequent spelling) that was picked up from the Arabic *hashishin*. The Arabic word was a nickname for a Muslim sect based in the mountains of Lebanon, under the leadership of an enigmatic "Old Man of the Mountains." Europeans became aware of the sect during the Crusades, and they brought back lurid and colorful stories about the *hashishiyy*. Some were true.

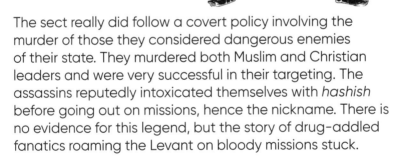

The sect really did follow a covert policy involving the murder of those they considered dangerous enemies of their state. They murdered both Muslim and Christian leaders and were very successful in their targeting. The assassins reputedly intoxicated themselves with *hashish* before going out on missions, hence the nickname. There is no evidence for this legend, but the story of drug-addled fanatics roaming the Levant on bloody missions stuck.

In the 14th century, Italian usage of the word became generalized to include any sort of assassin. This broadened sense made its way into French, and from there into the English vocabulary.

Baroque

Stylistically extravagant, ornamentally complex, grotesque; derived from the European dramatic style of art, architecture, and music from the 17th and 18th centuries.

....

The word *baroque* is now thrown around loosely to describe things that could more simply be called noticeably or overly complex. This sense has grown out of the slightly negative use of the word to mean "excessively elaborate or ornate." Originally, the word was limited to describing a prevailing artistic style that dominated western European culture in the realms of architecture, art, music, design, and other fields. Baroque was an older French word that stood for "irregularity," and once specifically only referred to pearls (or teeth) of unequal size or shape. This word in turn may have come from the Portuguese *barroco* ("imperfect pearl"), and be related to the Spanish *berruca* ("wart"). Since the baroque style later came to be viewed as contorted, overly ornamental, and even clumsy or pompous, the word itself came to acquire those connotations.

In its modern sense, the word often signifies an excessive or undesirable complexity. Some of the synonyms for the word offered by Merriam-Webster are telling: *devilish, excessive, extreme, immoderate, insane, intolerable,* and even *unconscionable.*

Hurricane

A massive storm (tropical cyclone) of exceptional destructive force in the western part of the Atlantic Ocean.

....

The infamous sea storm that seasonally threatens our Gulf Coast and Eastern Seaboard states takes its name from the Spanish *huracon* or *furacan*. Confronted with a cataclysmic weather event that the Spanish vocabulary had no word for, the early Spanish explorers adopted a local word (probably Arawakan, but the derivation is murky and contested). Initially, the word had a multitude of spellings that included *forcane, herrycano, harrycain,* and *hurlecane.*

Hurricanes are the same as the tropical cyclones that occur in other oceans of the world. They simply have a different traditional regional designation. All of these storms have the same characteristics: they begin as low pressure systems that form over warm tropical waters. Clusters of thunderstorms develop, and if they do not dissipate, may begin to rotate. If conditions are right, the rotating storms will grow in size, becoming a single, massive tropical cyclone. Its clouds draw moisture from the warm ocean. Depending on conditions, it can maintain or intensify its structure for days and move over the open water. Contact with land will lessen the intensity of a hurricane over time.

JULY 21

Dysphemism

A substitute word or phrase that is more negative or objectionable than the term it replaces.

....

While most people can identify a *euphemism* (the use of a less-offensive or neutral term in the place of a negative or taboo one), fewer people have heard of its opposite, a *dysphemism*. The Greek prefix *dys-* ("impaired, bad") is the opposite of *eu-* ("good"). Dysphemisms can make conversations more casual or be used for shock value. Many of the expressions heard in the military and other places where functional but unappealing food is served could be considered jocular dysphemisms. For example, army slang calls the ready-to-eat beef franks meal "the four fingers of death"; any drink made from powdered mix is called "bug juice."

JULY 22

Eidolon

An apparition or representative likeness, a phantom.

....

In ancient Greece, an *eidolon* was a spirit-image of a person, living or dead. The idea was not limited to Greek imagination—we find similar ideas in other cultures (for example, the Celtic *fetch*). The word entered English in the early 19th century as a poetic term from Greek mythology. But along the way, it came to imply something like "a likeness or unsubstantial image." That sense is now its primary meaning.

Artichoke

The immature flower head of a Mediterranean plant, having leaves that can be cooked and eaten.

When it first entered English (circa 1530), *artichoke* underwent a slew of creative spellings that included *archecokk*, *hortichock*, *artychough*, and *hartichoake*. The word comes to us in a roundabout way via the Italian *arcicioffo*, which comes from the Spanish *alcarchofa*, which derives from the Arabic *al-hursufa* (or *al-khurshuf*). Any way you look at it, the artichoke is quite a mouthful.

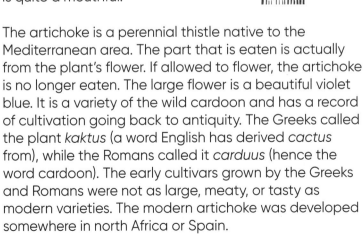

The artichoke is a perennial thistle native to the Mediterranean area. The part that is eaten is actually from the plant's flower. If allowed to flower, the artichoke is no longer eaten. The large flower is a beautiful violet blue. It is a variety of the wild cardoon and has a record of cultivation going back to antiquity. The Greeks called the plant *kaktus* (a word English has derived *cactus* from), while the Romans called it *carduus* (hence the word cardoon). The early cultivars grown by the Greeks and Romans were not as large, meaty, or tasty as modern varieties. The modern artichoke was developed somewhere in north Africa or Spain.

Triumph

As a noun, a victory; as a verb, to achieve victory.

Triumph comes to us from Latin. To the ancient Romans, a triumph was a parade celebrating a military victory. In the days of the Roman republic, generals were forbidden to enter the environs of Rome with their armies. The exception was after a major victory, when the senate granted the victors permission to ride through the streets of Rome, to the cheers of the entire city.

Roman poets also used the word *triumphus* to refer to a victory itself—as opposed to the post-battle ceremony—as did later prose writers in imperial Rome. But this sense was rare in Latin, and the word usually referred simply to the processional and accompanying celebrations.

Both of these senses were borrowed into English. There is one Old English work that uses the word: King Alfred's translation of the works of Orosius, a late Roman historian. But the word really makes its English appearance during the Renaissance, when classical culture was being studied. Today, the sense of the victory processional is still used in reference to Roman history, but the transferred sense of triumph meaning "victory, conquest" is the more usual English use.

Hallucinate

To have imaginary perceptions.

To *hallucinate* is to see something that isn't there, to perceive something illusory. The need for such a word in English was felt by 17th-century physician Sir Thomas Browne. He coined the word in 1646 from the Latin *alucinatus* ("to wander in the mind, dream, ramble in thought"). For Browne, the word meant a sort of "depraved" vision where things that don't exist are seen. Unfortunately, it proved to be a useful coinage.

Macrosmatic

Denoting a highly developed sense of smell.

Sure, it's a word with limited applications, but perhaps it's handy for zoologists and perfumers? Pigs, dogs, and sharks are *macrosmatic*. Humans are not—we're more the *microsmatic* sort of animal. While *micro* typically means "small," *macro* can mean "large" or "long." *Osmatic* has to do with the olfactory organs. English derives it from the French *osmatique*, a 19th-century coinage taken from the Greek root *osme* ("smell, scent, odor").

Goth

Now commonly referring to the subculture or music characterized by gloomy or morbid somberness, dark hair and clothes, and cultural touchpoints like horror films and Gothic literature; originally denoted a Germanic group north of the Roman Empire who invaded its territories in the early Christian era.

The definition of a *goth* really depends on who you ask. As part of the contemporary subculture, goths can be spotted by their dress. As music, it's all about the ambience. The term began circulating in the mid-1980s and described a postpunk music and fandom that favored a dramatic look that Bela Lugosi would have been proud of. The word itself was inspired by *gothic,* a 19th-century literary style that emphasized desolate landscapes and macabre violence. Think Mary Shelley's *Frankenstein*. Before the gothic literary style, there was the gothic style of art and architecture in the Middle Ages. The scholarly term was used for its general connotations of "Germanic, Teutonic," but really wasn't tied to the ancient Eastern European tribes who wreaked so much havoc upon the Mediterranean world.

Hybrid

Something which comes from diverse backgrounds, as in the offspring of two different breeds or subspecies of plant or animal.

Hybrid entered English in the 1600s with the restricted meaning of "offspring of plants or animals that come from different species or varieties." It was drawn from the Latin *hybrida* or *ibrida* ("mongrel, offspring of domesticated and wild pigs"). As a specialized term, it was rarely in general use. But in the mid-19th century, the meaning broadened to "product of two heterogeneous things." The meaning subsequently broadened further and may now be used in the sense of "being a blend of two distinct approaches, methods, or functions." That general definition is helpful in a contemporary world where creativity, inventiveness, and change are venerated. Hybrid workplaces, hybrid cars, and hybrid technologies are everywhere, and new hybrids are around the corner. As a noun, the word is increasingly being used as a shorthand reference to cars that use both electricity and gasoline.

Elastic

Capable of returning to an original form after being stretched or deformed; flexible or resilient quality.

English borrowed *elastick* from a French scientific term in the 1650s. Its first meaning was "having the property of recovering its former volume after compression" (referring to gases). The term was coined from the Latin *elasticus* and Greek *elastos* ("ductile, flexible"). It quickly came to reference a quality that could be present in other physical materials. By the mid-19th century, the stretchy nature of the word's primary meaning was exploited for figurative use and being applied to intangibles like concepts and emotional states.

Phosphene

An impression of light on the eye occurring when no light is actually present, usually caused by stimulation of the retina.

Vigorously rubbing your eyes in the dark may result in *phosphenes*. Those luminous streaks, swirls, and starbursts of color are the result of the cells of the retina being stimulated, whether from rubbing, violent coughing or sneezing, or even a blow to the head. The word is a 19th-century borrowing from French.

Aureate

Brilliantly golden in color; a highly ornamental style.

In Roman mythology, the goddess of the dawn was named *Aurora*. The Latin word for gold is *aurum*, with *aureas* meaning "golden." The *aur* part of these words is probably related to *aus* a Proto-Indo-European root whose core meaning is "to shine." From this lode of meanings we derive *aureole, auriferous, dorado, ore, oriole*—and *aureate*.

Though never commonly used, this word historically has shown up in literary contexts. From its primary meaning of "golden," it came to be used figuratively to indicate anything resplendent, whether in art, dress, or style of speech. From there, it acquired the slightly pejorative sense of "grandiloquent." Contemporary usage may have either positive or negative connotations—it might denote inspiring leadership qualities or an overblown speech or writing style. That said, it might be the perfectly ambiguous descriptor for something excessive or in need of a little fine tuning, as in, "I thought you gave the most aureate speech of the evening." Compliment or criticism?

AUGUST 1

Embarrass

Causing social unease or distress.

The modern meaning of *embarrass* has been around for about two centuries. Its earlier meaning of "to hamper or hinder," is no longer in common usage. The word entered English in the 16th century from the French *embarrasser* ("to block"), having circulated in other Romance languages like Spanish (*embarazar*), Italian (*imbarrazzo*), and Portuguese (*embaracar*). The double consonants of the word are a regular cause of spelling embarrassment.

AUGUST 2

Pannier

A large storage container, bag, or basket.

The all-purpose *pannier* is a handy word to have around to help us further differentiate between the various kinds of storage containers we need for all our stuff. A pannier can be the carrying basket loaded onto the back of an animal or person. It can be the bags attached to the sides of a bicycle or motorcycle. It can be a basket used for provisions. Up until the 19th century, it denoted large, hooplike contrivances attached to women's clothing, or a kind of overskirt. The word comes from Old French and Latin terms meaning "bread basket."

Bodega

A small grocery or convenience store located in an urban area.

Bodegas are a common sight in New York City, dotting many of the Big Apple's street corners. People from other parts of the country may not be familiar with the term though. The NYC institution goes back to post-WWII immigrants who began opening small convenience stores by the dozen. These entrepreneurs tended to be from the Caribbean, especially Puerto Rico and the Dominican Republic. These neighborhood shops carry a little of everything (just like what other parts of the country would call corner stores or party stores), like soap, detergent, toilet paper, beverages, chips, beer, convenience food, lottery tickets, and over-the-counter medicines. And unlike traditional grocery stores, many are open all night.

The word is Spanish, and once meant "a wine shop or wine cellar" (a meaning still in use in Spain), and is related to the Italian *bottega*. It comes from the Latin *apotheca* (like the word *apothecary*), which meant, "depot, storehouse." Another related word is the more upscale *boutique*.

AUGUST 4

Tabloid

A type of newspaper that presents material in compact format.

....

This word used to refer to a type of pill comprising several medicines compressed into one tablet and manufactured exclusively by the Burroughs, Wellcome and Company of Great Britain. However, in 1902, *The Westminster Gazette* won a court case to use the word, which the pharmaceutical company believed it owned. Strictly speaking, the term refers only to the size of a newspaper, and not its coverage; a tabloid is smaller than a standard broadsheet newspaper. Because the content of some of those tabloids was sensational, the term *tabloid journalism* came to have a negative connotation.

AUGUST 5

Admiral

A high-ranking officer in the Navy or Coast Guard.

....

Admiral was a title of rank adopted from Arabic-speaking ship captains who called themselves *Amir-al-bahl* ("commander of the sea"). In the U.S. Navy and Coast Guard, an admiral is a four-star commissioned officer who ranks immediately above a three-star vice admiral; the rank is equivalent to that of the four-star general of the Army, Air Force, or Marine Corps. There is one higher rank in the U.S. Navy, the five-star rank of fleet admiral, but that rank has not been awarded since World War II.

AUGUST 6

Dissimulate

Hiding a deception, deceiving in some way.

....

Dissimulate comes from the Latin *dissimulaten* ("to conceal under false appearances"). The root *simulare* means "to make similar to, imitate, copy." We typically use this word pejoratively: dishonest politicians, guilty court defendants, or slippery salesfolk all might be accused of dissimulating. The word's meaning has been roughly the same since the 16th century, suggesting a corresponding consistency in human behavior.

AUGUST 7

Autochthonous

Native or indigenous to a place by birth.

....

Autochthonous is an obscure, exotic-looking word that most of us will never need to say or spell, but it has undeniable word-nerd cachet. Whenever the need to verbally identify a creature as belonging to the environment it's found in arises, but *native, indigenous,* or *endemic* just won't do, autochthonous is your go-to choice. Even more obscure is the word's opposite, *allochthonous*— something originating in a place other than where it has been found.

Hubris

Great or exaggerated pride.

We know what it is when we see it: an excessive cockiness that seems to be asking for a comeuppance. *Hubris* is overconfidence that verges on the dangerous. The word is a back-formation from *hubristic*, and comes from the Greek *hybris* ("violence, insolence," and earlier, "presumption toward the gods"), and it was the Greeks who really developed the idea behind the word.

Think of the classic Greek myth of Icarus, son of maze-building Daedalus. In the well-known story, Icarus and his father fashion wings whose feathers are held together by wax. Daedalus warns his son not too fly too high, lest the sun's heat melts his wings. Icarus disobeys, flies too high, and plunges into the sea due to his heedless hubris. The Greeks believed hubris was a character flaw that led to disaster. The lesson of hubris is that the boundaries of human limitations should not be overstepped, lest catastrophe ensue.

AUGUST 9

Phrontistery

A place set aside for thinking or study.

. . . .

It doesn't surprise us that an erudite word like *phrontistery* traces back to an erudite Greek source. *Phrontistes* meant "philosopher" or "someone who thinks deeply," and comes from *phrontizein* ("to reflect upon, think about"). What's surprising is that the word was not originally used seriously. It was actually used by playwright Aristophanes to ridicule the school of Socrates.

AUGUST 10

Slumgullion

A meat stew.

. . . .

It's hardly fair to call this dish "culinary." The term sounds gross, and its etymology doesn't help matters. The word's origins aren't clear, but it is believed that *slum* derives from "slime," with *gullion* being an old word for "mud" or "stinking pit." In American English, it originally referred to a beverage and later came to be applied to a stew. What's in the stew? It depends on who you ask. For many, it's a beef, macaroni, and tomato dish that might also be called American Goulash. For others, pork, cabbage, carrots, or potatoes are involved. For yet others, it may feature seafood. From the beginning, cooks have been throwing every kind of ingredient into this stew—an apt approach for something called *slumgullion*.

Boss

Someone in charge of employees, a director or supervisor.

··

The general-purpose *boss* was adopted into colonial American English via the Dutch *baas*, a word of obscure origin. In the early 17th century, it was understood as the title of a Dutch ship's captain. Dutch was once spoken in the New York region when that area was a Dutch colony. As a loanword, it dates at least to the early 19th century, but undoubtedly was being used earlier. Sources tend to concur that the reason it was adopted was due to an egalitarian aversion to using *master*. That word already was used in association with slavery; boss provided a new word to indicate hierarchical rank.

That said, there really is no shortage of English words that get the idea across, including *captain, chief, coach, director, employer, executive, foreman, governor, head, kingpin, leader, manager, overseer, superintendent, supervisor* and *taskmaster*. Whether we like it or not, there seems to be a demand for multiple words to describe that bossy person who is bossing us around.

Honey

A sweet, sticky, syrup-like substance created from flower nectar by bees.

Honey is a very old word in the English language, tracing back to Old English *hunig*, and further, to a Proto-Germanic word *hunang*. It may be related to the Sanskrit *kancan*. In the Indo-European languages, the more common root word for honey is *melit*. Regardless of which word is used, terms to denote the substance tend to be old— as old as written history. References to honey can be found in the first cuneiform writings of the Middle East, the Old Testament, Homer's *Iliad*, and in the sacred literature of Egypt and India. There are laws about bees written into the Hittite code. At least one Mesolithic rock painting seems to show a person harvesting wild honey.

As a naturally-occurring sugar, honey was a valuable resource in earlier times. People revered the substance and it was a typical offering to local deities. Honey can be stored relatively easily without spoilage. In fact, archaeologists have often found pots of honey in ancient Egyptian tombs. Honey's indefinite shelf life would have been invaluable in earlier times when consistent access to food was less reliable.

AUGUST 13

Bailiwick

The district, office, or jurisdiction of a bailiff; a sphere of authority.

....

Bailiwick is a contraction of *baillifwik*, from the word *bailiff* (originally, a minor official that worked for a British sheriff). The first part of the word derives from the Latin *bajulare* ("to carry a burden"), while the ending *wick* is an older native word that once mean "village, dwelling place." Place names like Keswick, Norwich, and Smethwick all contain this root. The word now most commonly refers to a person's area of skill or expertise, similar to *wheelhouse*.

AUGUST 14

Derecho

A fast-moving line of storms with extremely powerful winds.

....

Derecho is a word that is unfortunately becoming more well known to Midwesterners as this storm type increases in frequency. In addition to high winds, these storm complexes generate tornados, heavy downpours, and flash floods. They are most common in Midwestern plains states like Iowa and Nebraska. The American Spanish word means "direct, straight ahead"—an apt description for these storms' quick and brutal ferocity.

Schadenfreude

The pleasure one feels when something bad happens to someone we dislike.

Borrowed directly from the German, *schadenfreude* is a compound of two German nouns, *Schaden* ("damage") and *Freude* ("joy"). It first showed up in German texts in the mid-1700s, and it made its way into English usage about a century later. While the word is usually lowercase, you will sometimes see it with an initial capital letter, following the German convention. You might also stumble across the later coinage *freudenschade,* which was modeled after the German word but doesn't actually exist in German. It describes that feeling of being miserable because of someone else's success.

WANGZUG?

Some other words borrowed from the German include *zugzwang,* a situation in a chess game where a player must make an undesirable move; *zugunruhe,* the urge to migrate, especially in captive birds; and *sprachgefühl,* which literally means "a feeling for language" and is used when someone has a good ear for language and knows what sounds correct or appropriate.

AUGUST 16

Sinister

Something that is evil or menacing.

· ·

We know a *sinister* villain when we see one: malevolent, threatening, and exuding ill-will. But while this definition is straightforward, the word's history is not. The Latin source word (also sinister) meant "on the left." Does this reveal a bias from right-hand-dominant society? Possibly. Compare this to the words derived from *dexter* (Latin for "right"): *dexterity* and *ambidextrous*. Both words have positive connotations. Not convinced there's a bias at play? Consider our next entry: *gauche*.

AUGUST 17

Gauche

Socially awkward, tactless, or crude.

· ·

The French source word *gauche* literally means "left." By an unfair extension, it has come to mean "clumsy, socially inexperienced, awkward." In fact, *awkward* once meant "left-handed." Left-handed people can't be blamed for thinking there's a linguistic conspiracy here. There's a lot of unproveable conjecture about how these words took on their lefty-bashing connotations. But unfortunately, multiple safety studies have shown that in a society generally designed for right-handers (think about car design, for example), lefties are more accident-prone than everyone else.

Undermine

To destroy by surreptitious means; to subvert something.

....

Undermine has an etymology that is readily apparent when examining its constituent elements: *under + mine.* The two elements are from different sources: Under is Old English, and mine is from the Anglo-Norman verb *miner,* meaning "to excavate beneath a wall or structure in order to collapse it." The Anglo-Norman word comes from the Latin *minare* ("to mine, to undermine"). The original senses of the English, French, and Latin verbs are all military in nature, in that the act denoted by the word indicated a belligerent purpose, with the sense of mine meaning "to extract minerals from the earth" coming shortly afterward. The English verb to undermine appears in the 14th century with the same meaning as the Anglo-Norman miner.

In English, the military senses of both undermine and mine coexisted for a fairly long period. But eventually the verb "to mine" ceased being used in the military sense and came to mean only "to dig or tunnel, to excavate." By the 15th century, undermine had taken on its current meaning.

AUGUST 19

Impeach

To charge a public official with a crime or breach of duty.

....

The word *impeach* has nothing to do with the fruit. It was first spelled *empeche* and comes from a Latin word meaning "entangle, ensnare." It is related to *impede* and first meant, like impede does today, "to hinder, prevent." Impede comes from a Latin word meaning "tie the feet together," and both impeach and impede are related to the Latin word for "foot."

Impeach took on the meaning of "to bring a charge against" in the 1300s, and it was another century before it began to be specifically applied to public officials. Many people today confuse impeachment—the bringing of the charge or accusation against a public servant or politician—with the determination of guilt or being convicted of a crime; impeachment, however, is only the beginning of the process. (Considering that many officials resign once impeached, this confusion is understandable.)

Impeach is also used to describe casting doubts on someone's credibility as a witness.

AUGUST 20

Furcate

Branching like a fork.

Furcate entered English in the 19th century via the Latin *furca* ("two-pronged fork, cloven"). The word can be further specialized as *bifurcate* or *trifurcate*. These words are often used in scientific and medical literature, but furcate is a handy word to describe what rivers, hiking trails, or roads often do.

AUGUST 21

Guy

A man.

Today the word *guy* is an accepted substitute for man or boy, but it came about in a less than positive manner. In the early 17th century, Guy Fawkes (1570–1606) was instrumental in a plan to blow up England's Parliament and kill King James I. Fawkes was captured and hanged, but people celebrated the day by carrying effigies of Guy throughout the streets. Anyone resembling Guy or his manner of dress became known as a guy. Guy Fawkes Night is still celebrated with bonfires and fireworks on November 5.

Notorious

Infamous; well-known.

While the word *notorious* is most commonly used today to describe something or someone that is well known for unenviable reasons, this hasn't always been the case.

Notorious is from the Latin word meaning "famous, well known," and it was adopted into English at the end of the 15th century in exactly this value-neutral sense. But very quickly it became associated with fame of an unsavory or infamous nature, and it underwent pejoration (adopting a negative meaning). The Church of England's *Book of Common Prayer* (1549), for example, uses the phrase "notorious synners." It was from oft-heard uses like this that notorious acquired its insalubrious reputation.

Despite the fact that the value-neutral notorious is still on the books (listed as the primary or secondary definition, depending on which dictionary you consult), usage experts typically advise against its use. Even so, we see professional writers using the word in exactly this sense.

Notoriety, a related word that has maintained a fairly inoffensive reputation, might have something to do with notorious's notorious tenacity in holding on to its neutral connotation.

AUGUST 23

Doppelgänger

A person's seeming twin or double from the spirit world.

....

Doppelgänger is a German word meaning "double goer" or "double walker." Essentially, a doppelgänger is defined as a person's twin, although certainly not in a genetic sense. Rather, a doppelgänger is often described as a very pale, almost bloodless version of the person. Its appearance usually means impending danger or even death for its human counterpart, although there have been instances in which the doppelgänger foretold the future or simply showed up and didn't cause any harm.

AUGUST 24

Ersatz

An imitation or substitution that is of inferior quality.

....

Ersatz is a German loanword that entered English in the 1870s, and had the sense of "substitute." It gained popularity during World War I, when it was specifically used to mean "an inferior imitation" (as in products made from inferior materials or substances due to wartime rationing). An ersatz coffee might be one heavily cut with chicory, for example. The privations of World War II helped to further cement this usage.

Gossip

As a noun, both a person who talks extensively about other people's personal business and the rumors that are spread; as a verb, to relate gossip.

Once an approved manner of discussing someone's business, the word *gossip* came from the religious rite of baptism. Those adults who stand up for a baby during the ceremony are known as godparents. The godparents of one child were considered "related" to the godparents of another child in that family and became known to each other as "godsibb." These insiders were given the right to discuss family business among themselves. A little too much discussion might have made way for a broader definition of "godsibb," or "gossip" to mean people who tell tales, spreading both truth and rumor.

While it's perfectly acceptable to refer to someone who gossips by the simple term gossip (as in, "she's such a gossip that I never tell her anything"), you might also use the terms *gossiper* and *gossipmonger* for those who spread chatty talk about other people.

AUGUST 26

Scrofulous

Afflicted with scrofula or appearing unwell.

....

Scrofula is a tubercular disease of the lymph nodes. The Latin source word literally means "little pigs." To appear scrofulous therefore, can mean having a diseased look. But the word's meaning has acquired a pejorative sense, and contemporary usage may denote something morally reprehensible about the thing or person described.

AUGUST 27

Solander

A protective case for books, documents, or art objects, typically book-shaped.

....

Solander is an eponym. The person in this case was Daniel Solander, a Swedish 18th-century botanist. He developed a special protective case for storing archival materials, the solander box, while he worked at the British Museum, from 1763 to 1782. Solanders are box-like enclosures made of wood, leather, fabric, felt, or other materials. The flexible joints of the construction allow it to be opened and closed without damaging the protected materials inside.

IT'S EPONYMOUS

....

Here are just a few other eponyms lurking in our English vocabulary: *bloomers, braille, cardigan, diesel, leotard, lynch, maverick, mesmerize, poinsettia, scrooge, shrapnel, volt,* and *watt.*

AUGUST 28

Schlep

To move from one place to another, especially to haul something.

Schlep means to drag or haul something that's especially burdensome, or to make a tedious journey: "No one will help me schlep my stuff to my new apartment." A schlep can also refer to someone who is a drag: "He's such a schlep." Schlep comes from the Yiddish word *shlepn*, which means "to drag," and before that from German. Shlep and shlepp are variant spellings. The word first started appearing in English sources in the early 20th century.

AUGUST 29

Heirloom

Something of value passed down in a family through generations.

The first instance of this word, as *ayre lome*, was recorded in 1472, in England and perhaps Scotland. It later became the separate words *heir* and *loom*. Interestingly, the latter didn't necessarily have to do with the textile business. Loom was a word that encompassed all implements, household items, tools, and other personal items, and in fact comes from an Old English word *geloma*, meaning "tool." In agriculture, heirloom varieties of plants are grown by seeds that were saved and passed down, instead of through use of modern cultivars. To qualify as an heirloom cultivar, it must be at least 50 years old, though some would argue at least a century old.

Gourmet

As a noun, someone who appreciates and is able to judge quality, especially in food and drink; as an adjective, describing quality food, drink, or dining.

The term *gourmet* has made its way up in the world. From the French, it originally referred to a horse groom, then to minor household servants who tasted the wine for quality. In time, this position at a wine shop was used to refer to a connoisseur of fine wines. This led to the modern meaning of one who prefers, can distinguish, or can create fine food and drink, a meaning that developed in the first half of the 19th century. The adjective form started appearing around a century later.

GOURMAND

A related term from the same root is *gourmand*, someone who enjoys and appreciates eating good food, especially in large quantities. Gourmand actually appears earlier in English, dating back to the 15th century. While today it's primarily used descriptively, it once carried decidedly negative connotations of gluttony and greed.

AUGUST 31

Cornucopia

An exceptionally fruitful abundance.

Originally, a *cornucopia* was a very specific, tangible thing: a curved, hollow goat's horn that had been filled to overflowing with fruits, vegetables, and other objects associated with a successful, abundant harvest. The Latin *cornu copiae* meant "horn of plenty" (*cornu* is related to our "horn," and *copiae* is the root of "copious"). The idea came from mythology, specifically the story of the goat Amalthea who nurtured the infant Zeus. For the Greeks and Romans, the horn of plenty was a traditional symbol of abundance, and appeared in art and architecture.

GODDESS OF PLENTY

Copious comes from a Latin word meaning "abundant supply." *Copia* was also the name of a minor Roman goddess. She represented wealth and plenty, and was often seen carrying a cornucopia.

The word first appeared in English in the early 16th century. Usage gradually became more figurative, with the sense "source of abundance" eventually becoming its most common meaning.

Grouch

A bad-tempered or irritable person.

GROUCHES EVERYWHERE

Grouch represents another one of those subjects that the English language seems to have a predilection for. If that word doesn't hit quite the right tone, consider *complainer, crab, crank, curmudgeon, doomsayer, fatalist, grinch, grouser, grump, killjoy, spoilsport, sourpuss,* or *whinger.*

Grouch showed up in American English in the 1890s, when people began complaining about "having a grouch on." It apparently grew from college student slang, but the word's origins are unclear. It might be an alteration of *grutching* ("complaint"), or *grudge.* Though it was originally used only as a noun, active Americans saw the need to throw their bad moods around more vigorously, and by 1916 it was being used as a verb. People have been grouching ever since.

Grouch bag dates to 1908 and means "small bag containing money concealed on one's person." This was possibly the source of Groucho Marx's name. He was known to carry just such a bag to poker games.

SEPTEMBER 2

Eavesdrop

To listen to a private conversation by surreptitious means.

Why is snooping on someone's conversation called *eavesdropping*? At one time, landholders weren't allowed to build right up against a property line—they had to leave room between their space and that of the neighbors for the eaves on the house, as well as for water dripping from rainy weather. An *eavesdrip* was only about 24 inches, a small enough space for a curious neighbor to easily hear what went on next door—whether he or she wanted to or not. The word began to be used in its current meaning in the early 1600s.

SEPTEMBER 3

Checkmate

In chess, to leave an opponent's king with no route for escape, thus winning the game; the term can also be used figuratively.

The game of chess originated in Asia, with the earliest forerunner probably appearing in India, and evolved as it moved from one country to another. *Shatranj*, as it was known in Persia, added a game piece to represent a king. The objective was to capture the opponent's king, with players exclaiming *Shāh Māt*—Persian for "the king is helpless" —when attack was imminent. As the game gained popularity in other lands, players continued the tradition of announcing their fatal game blows. In Arabic, the exclamation used was *sheikh-mat*, which, over time, became the well-known *checkmate*.

Flummox

To confound.

Unfortunately, searching for the etymology of the word *flummox* will flummox you. We know this piece of British slang arose in the first half of the 19th century, but not much more than that. One early use is found in Charles Dickens's 1837 work The *Pickwick Papers*. A character named Mr. Weller says, "Verever he's a-goin' to be tried, my boy, a alleybi's the thing to get him off. Ve got Tom Vildspark off that 'ere manslaughter, with a alleybi, ven all the big vigs to a man said as nothing couldn't save him. And my 'pinion is, Sammy, that if your governor don't prove a alleybi, he'll be what the Italians call reg'larly flummoxed, and that's all about it."

Despite Mr. Weller's words, no one suggests that flummox came from the Italian language. One reasonable but unproven theory is that the word came from a regional English term, *flummock*, a person who's a bit of a klutz.

Sobriquet

A moniker or epithet.

....

The word *sobriquet*, or *soubriquet*, was picked up directly from the identical French term of the same meaning. It appeared in English circa 1640. In Middle French, the word had an additional meaning, referring to an affectionate chuck under someone's chin, but only the sense of "nickname" made it over to England.

The field of sports is a rich one for creative sobriquets. In some cases, these nicknames are so well known that casual watchers of the sport either never learned or might find it difficult to remember a player's birth name. Golfer Tiger Woods, for example, goes exclusively by "Tiger" instead of his legal name Eldrick, and basketball legend Earvin Johnson is more popularly known as "Magic." Some sobriquets rely on rhyming or wordplay, like basketball's Wilt "the Stilt" Chamberlain or runner Usain Bolt's "Lightning Bolt." Others act as hype or a warning to opponents, like Wayne Gretzky's "The Great One" or defensive lineman Walter Perry's "The Fridge." (No one wants to be hit by a refrigerator.) And some names continue to live on in history, like Babe Ruth's "The Sultan of Swat" or Willie Mays's "The Say Hey Kid."

SEPTEMBER 6

Candy

As a noun, crystallized sugar; a sweet treat made with sugar; something pleasing ("eye candy"); as a verb, to coat with sugar.

In Persian, the word for sugar was *qand*. It transitioned to Arabic as *qandi*, to Old French as *sucre candi*, and then to Middle English as *sugre candy*. The verb form started to appear around 1530. Though now we think of candied fruit as more of a treat, the process was also an important way to preserve food.

SEPTEMBER 7

Jargon

Language that obscures meaning; terminology associated with a specific activity or field that may be impenetrable to outsiders.

The word dates back to the 14th century: *Jargon* is an Old French word for the incomprehensible and meaningless chattering of birds, and it made the leap from there to describe human speech that's difficult to understand. Jargon may simply refer to technical or specialized terms that are useful and precise in context. Sports fans, cooking enthusiasts, and scientific experts may all happily use jargon in their chosen arena. Jargon can, however, be purposefully obscure as well, meant to exclude and even trick someone.

Flamingo

A bird from the family *Phoenicopteridae.*

When Spanish and Portuguese explorers encountered these fascinating aquatic birds in the 1560s, they applied the word *flamengo* to them. Literally, the word means "flame-colored." Some etymologies trace the word ultimately to the Latin *flamma* ("flame") via a Provençal intermediary. However, the Spanish *flamengo* has also been tied to *flamenco*, which literally referred to a Fleming, or native of Flanders, before it became known as the dance. Different sources list different reasons for the tie; some point toward the reddish complexion of people from Flanders; some to their colorful clothing.

Flamingos (or flamingoes) are not born pink. They are initially grayish-red, becoming entirely pink or even deep red over time, based on the carotenoids in their diet of algae, shrimp, and plankton. Birds that don't get enough carotenoids to sustain their color can lose color and turn pale; this is often a sign of ill health.

PINK FACT

The bird's scientific name *Phoenicopteridae* also refers to its color. It's a combination of the Greek words for "red" or "crimson" and "feather."

Pelf

Wealth; money; often used to refer specifically to ill-gotten gains.

The Old French word *pelfre*, referring to wealth gained by piracy or theft, became an Anglo-French term *pelf* that ultimately gave us two English words: the noun *pelf* and the verb *pilfer* ("to steal, usually in small amounts"). Pelf showed up in the late 1300s. Over time, the word lost some of its criminal connotation, but it can definitely still be used to refer to wealth or property acquired by unsavory means. Pelf, like booty and loot, doesn't have a plural form.

OTHER PILFERINGS

Pilfer arrived in English as a verb in the 1540s and is only used as a verb nowadays, but it had previously been used as a noun, equivalent to pelf. Today, the related noun *pilferage* refers to the theft, while *pilferer* is used to refer to the thief. A company might try to pilfer-proof its pilferable items to reduce pilferage by pilferers.

Amok

Out of control; in a frenzy, potentially a violent or murderous one.

When a crowd of people begins to physically panic, it is said to "run amok." The phrase entered the English language during the 17th century and comes from the Malay word *amok*, which means "violent and out of control." The phrase "run amok" corresponded to the Malay verb *megamok*. In Malay, and in its early English language use, the noun by itself indicated a murderous frenzy, a state in which a person might go berserk and commit mass murder. Today, we generally use the adverb form, almost always in conjunction with the phrase "run" or "ran," and it tends to be used more figuratively and in a playful sense.

People can run amok, but the word can also be used to describe other creatures or situations that get out of control. For example, you might say, "Inflation cannot be allowed to run amok."

Guild

A group or association, especially of tradespeople.

The word *guild* showed up as guilds were rising in power in parts of Europe in the 1300s. While associations of merchants and artisans had formed before that point, guilds became very common in the Middle Ages. Generally, you had to join a guild in order to practice your craft within a specific city, although not all cities were associated with guilds. Guilds established standards for their members, and often set up defined career paths from apprentice to journeyman to master.

The Middle English spelling was *gilde* (and *gild* is still an acceptable variant spelling today), which derived from an Old Norse term, *gildi* ("payment"). Related words were the Old English *gegield* ("brotherhood"), the Old Saxon *geld* ("payment"), the Old High German *gelt* (payment or sacrifice), and the Proto-German *geldja* ("payment").

YIELD

An etymologically related term is *yield*, in the sense of production. ("The investment should yield a good return.")

SEPTEMBER 12

Flunky

A servant; an underling or low-level employee; a sycophant.

....

When the term *flunky* showed up circa 1782 in Scotland, it referred to a liveried, or uniformed, servant. A servant might need to flatter or agree with their employer to stay on their employer's good side, and by 1855 the term was being used to refer to anyone who obsequiously agreed with a more powerful person, and had acquired dismissive and derogatory overtones. *Flunkey* and *flunkie* are acceptable variant spellings.

SEPTEMBER 13

Hijack

To steal goods as they are in transit; to take over a vehicle; to take over a process or conversation.

....

The word *hijack* appeared in the United States sometime between 1918 and 1923. Though it appeared quite recently in the historical record, its origins aren't clear. Most people suspect it came from a straightforward combination of *highway* and *jack* (in the sense, "to steal"). The term was first used in connection with aircraft in the late 1960s, although the first actual aircraft hijacking had happened decades earlier. Airplane hijackings did, however, increase in the late 1950s and throughout the 60s, and although someone coined *skyjack* in the early 1960s, it never really took off.

Emoji

An icon or symbol used in digital communication formats to represent an emotion or an object.

The word *emoji* first showed up in 1997, from a straightforward combination of the Japanese words for "picture" (*e*) and "character" (*moji*). It was picked up in English circa 2008 as operating systems in the Western world adopted emojis. The term emoticon—where the user creates something like a smiley face from existing keyboard characters—had showed up in English in the late 1980s. Though it sounds similar, it derives from an English mashup of emotion and icon.

Nickname

As a noun, an epithet; a familiar, usually shortened, form of one's name; as a verb, to nickname.

Around 1300, the word *ekename* started to appear in Middle English. *Eke* was related to the Old English *eaca* ("increase"). an ekename was literally an additional name. As happened with several Middle English words, the word and its article were combined differently over time. That is, an ekename became a *nekename*, and that spelling was in use by the mid-1400s. (A *newt*, incidentally, started off as *an ewt*.) Eventually nekename shifted further to nickname. The word began being used as a verb about 1530.

Clue

As a noun, a hint; evidence; an idea or insight; as a verb, to provide a hint.

Let's see if we can untangle this labyrinthine etymology. The spelling of *clue* first showed up in English in the mid-1400s; before that, the word was spelled *clew*. At that time, though, a clew was a physical object, a ball of yarn. The word came from an Old English word for ball that was picked up from a Proto-Germanic word for ball. In the late 1500s and early 1600s, clue picked up a symbolic

meaning. In mythology, the story of the Minotaur relates how Ariadne gave Theseus a ball of yarn to guide him out of labyrinth. The word for a literal ball of thread thus was adapted to describe figurative threads of insight.

The verb form, usually phrased as "clue in" or "clued in" showed up with that meaning later, in the first half of the 20th century.

GET A CLUE

The movie *Clueless* was released in 1995, but the word appeared much earlier. One source finds a mid-18th century usage where it meant "lacking clues."

Radical

Different from normal or usual, in an extreme sense.

Radical entered the English vocabulary in the 14th century as a word whose primary meaning had to do with something coming from the ground or having roots. It came from the Latin *radicalis* ("having roots"), which in turn derived from *radix* ("root"). The Latin word looks similar to our *root*, and is, in fact, cognate to the English word, sharing the Proto-Indo-European wrad. Words derived from this root include *eradicate, licorice, radish, ramada, ramus, rhizoid, rhizome, rutabaga,* and *wort*.

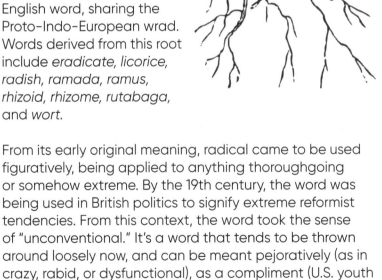

From its early original meaning, radical came to be used figuratively, being applied to anything thoroughgoing or somehow extreme. By the 19th century, the word was being used in British politics to signify extreme reformist tendencies. From this context, the word took the sense of "unconventional." It's a word that tends to be thrown around loosely now, and can be meant pejoratively (as in crazy, rabid, or dysfunctional), as a compliment (U.S. youth slang for admirable, in a slightly out-of-control way), or disruptively cutting-edge.

Ketchup

A saucy condiment made from tomatoes.

....

This condiment would have been unrecognizable in its earlier incarnations, especially as a fish-based sauce. But as a matter of fact, that's how it got its name.

Back around 1700, the Malay name for this sauce was *kichap*, from the Chinese Amoy dialect's *koechiap*, or "brine of fish." Early English versions of the condiment included mushrooms, walnuts, cucumbers, and oysters. The modern form of the condiment began when New Englanders added tomatoes. (One recipe from the 1800s included both tomatoes and anchovies, providing a link from the fish of the past to the tomatoes of today.) Standard recipes today include tomatoes, a sweetening agent such as sugar or corn syrup, vinegar, and various spices.

Catsup (earlier, catchup) is a less common variant spelling that is used in some portions of the United States. In the United States, tomato sauce is a separate entity from ketchup, but in other countries you might hear ketchup referred to as tomato sauce or red sauce.

Bloviate

A breezy, windy manner in speech or writing.

....

Bloviate has American Midwestern slang origins. The word dates back to around the 1850s. It seems to have been a joining of *blow* with the *-ate* ending (modelled after *deviate*). It originally had a meaning along the lines of "time spent idly chatting" or sometimes "boastful talk." The word was becoming obsolete in the early 20th century when the presidency of Warren G. Harding resurrected it. Harding used the word occasionally (in a neutral sense), and this usage was noted. Harding was a verbose speech-giver, and henceforward verbosity became associated with the word.

Cappuccino

A beverage of espresso and frothed milk or cream.

....

This word is a recent direct borrowing from the Italian word. *Cappuccino* derives from *Capuchin*, the name denoting the religious order associated with St. Francis. The coffee drink draws its name from the distinctive brown robes worn by Franciscan friars. The derivative word *capuccio* means "hood" in Italian.

Opulence

Significant wealth or affluence.

....

Opulence entered English in the early 1600s via the identically-spelled French word. The French word comes from *opulentus* ("abounding in resources"). Unlike *wealth, means, capital, riches, substance,* or *fortune,* opulence has a shade of meaning that implies an elevated lifestyle or thoughtful luxury, not just money in the bank. Furnishings, art objects, interior decorating, or the grounds of a property all might be described as opulent.

There's an irony contained in the etymology of opulence. Its Proto-Indo-European root *op* connotes "work, production, labor"—something that those who can afford opulence need not worry much about. Other words that derive from this root include *cooperate, copious, copy, oeuvre, office, opera, operate, optimism,* and *opus.*

Hobo

An itinerant homeless person.

....

First heard in the American Pacific Northwest in the late 1800s, the term differentiated migrants who were willing to work from "bums" or "tramps," who would not. The term *hobo* itself is possibly slang for "Ho boy," "Hello Brother," or even "hoe-boy" (an itinerant farm worker). By the 1890s, hobo was an accepted term, a fraternity growing in tandem with the miles of railroad tracks springing up across the United States. Hobos became particularly iconic during the Great Depression.

SEPTEMBER 23

Conflate

To blend, confuse, or blur together.

....

Originally, the mid-15th-century borrowing from Latin meant "create from a mold or cast from metal." The Latin *conflatus* (past participle of *conflare*) meant "melt together" or "blow up, kindle." That sense is now obsolete. The meaning "mix from different sources" is from the early 17th century. In modern usage, *conflate* usually means "to mix up with."

Avatar

Incarnation (as of a deity) in human form; embodiment of an idea; a digital image (as in a video game) meant to represent someone.

Once a fairly uncommon word, *avatar* has seen a rise in usage thanks to a blockbuster movie and the adoption of the word in digital and online formats. It comes from a Sanskrit word (*avatarah*) which means "descent of a deity into worldly form." It entered English in this specific sense in the late 18th century. By the next century, its meaning had broadened to "concrete embodiment of an idea, concept, or philosophy."

The 2009 film *Avatar* brought the word even more publicity, as well as a very specific context for its use. In the film, humans remotely operate hybrid-alien bodies via psionic brain link. This sense echoes the original meaning of the word. Even more significant is the growth of a new meaning which is probably the one used by most people now—the graphical representation of a person online or in a video game format. This kind of avatar may have a two-dimensional form and appear as a simple icon (as seen in online communities), or appear as a three-dimensional form (as in virtual worlds or video games).

Eponym

One for whom something is named.

....

The ending *-nym* means "name," from the Greek, so *homonym* means "same name," *pseudonym* means "false name," and *synonym* means "together name" (two words that, together, name the same thing). When you think of an *eponym*, think of having your "name on" something, since the Greek *epo-* means "on, upon." In "Max's Restaurant," Max is an eponym.

Eponyms often mark the most enduring human accomplishments and afflictions. Astronomer Edmond Halley, a contemporary and friend of Isaac Newton, calculated the orbit period of the comet that is now eponymously called Halley's Comet. The element einsteinium wasn't actually discovered by Einstein, but the name is a tribute to the great thinker. Even the Fosbury Flop, the backward high jump technique introduced by jumper Dick Fosbury, honors a pioneer.

Some eponyms are for distinctions no one aspires to. Lou Gehrig was a Hall of Fame baseball player, but his name might be best known for the disease he suffered from and ultimately succumbed to: amyotrophic lateral sclerosis (ALS), or Lou Gehrig's disease.

Patriot

A person loyal to their country and often willing to defend it against enemies.

. . . .

The word's Greek origin, *patris*, means "of one's father." In the 16th century, the French used the word *patriote* to mean fellow countryman. In the 17th century, a good *patriot* loved his country and supported the government. Later, the word was used to describe people who professed loyalty to Great Britain, but were actually anti-government. By the 18th century, Benjamin Franklin used the word to define American colonists seeking their freedom.

The French Canadian people used the word to describe a political movement called the Patriote Rebellion at the turn of the 19th century. The patriotes were inspired by the American Revolution and demanded an elected council instead of one appointed by Great Britain. Today the word is used positively. For example, Desmond Tutu was called a "patriot without equal" by *People Magazine* in 2021. Patriot is also the name of a type of missile developed in Alabama and used by the U.S. Army, and by other country's armed forces. It's an acronym for "**p**hased **a**rray **t**racking **r**adar to **i**ntercept **o**n **t**arget."

SEPTEMBER 27

Umpire

A sports official who makes decisions on what plays are valid; to referee.

The term *umpire* derives from the 14th-century Middle English word *noumpere*. It evolved over the years to *oumpere* and finally to *nonper*, where the word breaks down into two parts: *non* for "not" and *per* for "equal." In short, the word signified "not an equal." It was used to describe the third man called in to settle disagreements. Interestingly, that is why there are an uneven number of umpires in sports—so that someone always has the deciding vote.

SEPTEMBER 28

Obsecration

An earnest prayer, supplication, or entreaty.

As *obsecracioun* ("prayer, entreaty") this word entered English in the late 14th century. Its meaning has remained relatively unchanged since. The Latin root *sacrare* ("to make sacred") is cognate with *sacred*. To *obsecrate* is to beg or supplicate. The word most frequently appears in religious contexts.

SEPTEMBER 29

Tenebrous

Dark, murky, or obscure.

The Old French word *tenebros* meant "dark or gloomy."
It entered English with this sense in the 15th century. The
word traces back to the Latin *tenebrae*, which had a very
similar meaning (essentially, "darkness"). We might speak
of tenebrous depths, a tenebrous period of history, or even
a tenebrous state of mind. There is also a style of painting
known as *tenebrism*, associated with the Italian painter
Caravaggio and his adherents, that makes dramatic use of
darkness, shadow, and intense illumination.

SEPTEMBER 30

Azimuth

An angular measurement in a spherical coordinate system;
a calculated arc of the horizon or horizontal direction,
useful in astronomy and navigation.

This borrowing from the late 14th century comes from the
French and Latin *azimut* via an Arabic word (*as-sumut*)
meaning "the ways" or "directions." Quite a few other
European languages have also borrowed the word. Its first
appearance in a European language was in Spanish, in an
astronomy book based on Arabic sources. It first appeared
in English in Chaucer's *Treatise on the Astrolabe.*

Celerity

Speed, haste, fast action; a term to describe the velocity of a wave.

Celerity comes from an early French word, *celerite*, and the Latin word, *celeritas*, meaning quickness and speed. The word's Greek root, *keles*, means runner, racer, or fast ship. The word appeared in English in the 15th century.

The word was used in both literary and scientific contexts. Shakespeare wrote "Celerity is never more admired than by the negligent," while 19th-century Englishman Sir John Astley, said "Celerity wins the race." On the scientific side, Benjamin Franklin used "celerity" to mean velocity.

The word's use has declined since the middle 1800s, although it popped up in W. Somerset Maugham's 1915 novel, *Of Human Bondage*, when he wrote about an undertaker's window display reading, "Economy, Celerity, Propriety," next to some coffins. Today, scientists use it in the phrase, "wave celerity." They use complicated formulas to determine the celerity of an ocean wave, for example.

OCTOBER 2

Paparazzi

Photographers who aggressively follow celebrities in order to take photos of them.

Though often confused in popular usage, *paparazzi* is actually the plural of *paparazzo*. The paparazzi are the most tenacious—celebrities would say obnoxious—of photographers. Their reputation for stealthy stalking behavior is legitimately deserved. The word itself comes from the Italian surname of a fictional photographer in the 1959 film *La Dolce Vita*. The behavior of these types of photographers was known internationally by this time. By the end of the 1960s, the term was being widely used as a word for intrusive photographers.

OCTOBER 3

Tacky

Sticky or adhesive; in bad taste.

Tacky is an 18th-century shortening of *tack*, and initially took its sense of "act of attaching temporarily" from that word (as in "tack a poster to the wall"). As a word meaning "in bad taste," its meaning grew out of a mid-19th-century sense of "shabby, seedy," which in turn grew from "neglected horse." The definition was later extended to mean anything cheap, vulgar, inferior, or in poor condition.

Imbroglio

An embarrassing misunderstanding, confused situation, scandal, or complicated altercation.

That complicated tangle of embarrassing events, misunderstood scenarios, or scandalous goings-on known as *imbroglios* can be comic or tragic. Sitcoms regularly feature imbroglios, as do military campaigns and corporate maneuverings. An imbroglio is something more enjoyable to watch than participate in.

The word came into English from the Italian *imbrogliare* ("confuse, tangle") around 1750, and initially had the primary sense of "a jumble." By the 19th century, it had acquired its modern meaning. The Italian word was taken from the French word *embrouiller*. If this word looks similar to *embroil*, that's because the English word is derived from this source too. So these two synonyms—embroil and imbroglio—both derive from the same French word. It's appropriate that the French source word *brouiller* means "confuse or mix." It comes from an older French word meaning "broth." So you might say that to be in an imbroglio is to be "in the soup."

OCTOBER 5

Cretin

A loutish, stupid, insensitive, or idiotic person.

....

Whether or not it's true that French has provided us with more insult words than any other language, this French borrowing is certainly pungently offensive. But there's a surprising twist to this word's etymology. *Cretin* comes from a word in the French Alpine dialect, *crestin*. Parts of the region did not naturally provide enough iodine for local diets, and this caused thyroid problems in some of the local population. The word crestin referred to people afflicted with a congenital thyroid deficiency. Crestin had the sense of "victim, poor fellow," and was actually a derivation of *christian.* So in its initial sense, the word was commiserative and sympathetic.

OCTOBER 6

Desuetude

Discontinuance of a practice, exercise, fashion, or regular use.

....

Desuetude comes from a mid-15th-century borrowing from the Latin word *desuetudo* ("disuse"). The Latin root *suescere* meant "becoming accustomed," and indirectly provided us with the word *custom*. Desuetude may be an infrequently used word these days, but it hasn't fallen into desuetude just yet.

Orrery

A mechanical solar system model popularized in the 1700s.

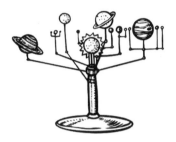

In the 1700s, Irish essayist Sir Richard Steele dubbed a mechanical device with a globe at the center representing the sun and the planets an *orrery*. He named it after Charles Boyle, the Earle of Orrery, who had commissioned clockmakers to create the device. It contained a handle that could be turned to imitate the relative periods of rotation of the planets around the sun. Orreries were popular then and used for education as well as home recreation. The philosopher and artist Joseph Wright of Derby gave lectures on the orrery in the 1700s and also drew a painting of people gazing at this representation of the heavens.

Digital orreries, viewed on computers with special software, have now taken over from the mechanical ones once used for studying the universe. But people can still see some of the old ones at museums. Scientists recently built the world's largest orrery at the University of Manchester's School of Physics and Astronomy in England, where it has become a tourist attraction. Today, there's even a human orrery in Ireland where people play the roles of the sun, planets and comets.

Treacle

Molasses; something that is overly sweet; obsolete: an antidote.

....

Treacle is the British English word for molasses, but it and its adjectival form, *treacly,* refer to anything that is sickeningly sweet or sentimental. Before treacle referred to molasses, though, it was used to refer to a medicine—specifically, an antidote for poison—and its etymological roots come from that usage. The word treacle was a form of *theriac* or *theriaca*, meaning a medical cure-all, especially of animal venom. Those words derived from the Latin *theriaca*, in turn deriving from the Greek *thēriakē*, which referred to a medicine used as an antidote for poisonous animal bites.

Molasses itself is a syrupy byproduct made when sugar is extracted and refined. Its name also comes from the Latin—in this case, *mel,* the Latin word for honey.

Blitz

An air raid; an aggressive football play in which extra members of the defense (which typically remain behind the line of scrimmage) rush the opposing team's vulnerable quarterback; an intensive, time-sensitive campaign.

Blitzing is as inherent to football as goalposts and concussions, but the word itself didn't originate with the game. Like many terms—*deadline* and *AWOL*, for example—it has military origins. The word is derived from the German *blitzkrieg* (literally "lightning war"), defined by the *Oxford English Dictionary* as "an attack or offensive launched suddenly with great violence with the object of reducing the defenses immediately." It wasn't long before the shortened version of the term found its way into the lexicon of America's favorite rough-and-tumble pastime.

While war buffs and sports fans might most readily associate the word blitz with a literal exertion of force, the term has enjoyed what linguists call semantic broadening, making it useful for those of us who occupy ourselves with more civil diversions. Like other sports terms—*home run* and *slam dunk*, for example—blitz can be used in a figurative sense. Consequently, we might refer to a new ad campaign as a marketing blitz.

Petrichor

The smell of rain, especially after it's been dry and warm.

Humans have long noticed the pleasant, earthy smell of rain, often after a dry spell. Some even claim they can detect that distinct odor even before rain begins. The smell was called argillaceous odor until 1964 when Australian scientists coined the word *petrichor*. Petrichor comes from two Greek words, *petra* ("rock") and *ikhor*, referring to the blood of mythological gods.

Scientists determined that when rain water interacts with plant oils contained in rocks and soil, a compound called *geosmin* is released. It's the geosmin that has the pleasant, musky odor. A human nose can detect geosmin in the air even in very small quantities. Scientists later discovered that micro-organisms called actinobacteria become more active when it rains, which creates more geosmin.

Petrichor can occur just before it rains, when the humid air moistens the ground and starts releasing the geosmin. That's what's happening when someone says they can smell rain coming. When the rain stops, the ground dries and the petrichor goes away. But it's something to look forward to on another rainy day.

Cesarean

A surgical procedure to deliver a baby by cutting through the walls of the abdomen.

Cesarean is a 1903 shortened, Americanized version of the term *caesarian section* (first used in 1615), an operation that was purportedly named after Gaius Julius Caesar, who was supposedly delivered by this method (legend traces his name to the Latin *caesus,* from *caedere,* which means "to cut"). This detail of Caesar's birth, however, may not be entirely accurate, as such operations in ancient times were inevitably fatal to the mother, and history shows that Caesar's mother did not die in childbirth.

Audit

An examination of finances; to review something; to attend a course without the intent of pursuing credit.

The prefix *audi–* comes from the Latin *audire,* or "to hear," and is used in a number of English words related to sound, such as *auditorium, audible,* and *audience.* Back in the day, relatively few written records were kept, and a financial *audit* usually consisted of questioning witnesses about their accounts and listening to their responses. This early use of audit in English dates to 1435.

Lagniappe

A small thank-you gift from a merchant to a customer; any extra or unexpected benefit.

Mark Twain discovered a new word when he visited New Orleans in the late 1800s. In his book, *Life on the Mississippi*, he called it a "nice, limber, expressive, handy word." He often heard people saying, "Give me something for *lagniappe*." It might be a piece of licorice root given to a child who buys candy or an extra doughnut when a customer buys a dozen.

Lagniappe comes from the South American Spanish phrase *la yapa*, which means a free extra item. The word came into the English language in New Orleans, via the French Creoles, who had learned it from Spanish-speaking neighbors. The practice of giving a lagniappe is used in other places in the United States with similar cultural influences. It also is common in Hispanic nations as well as in North Africa, France, Holland, and Switzerland. In Peruvian markets today, customers may ask for la yapa and receive a little extra from the vendors. Street vendors in Louisiana are expected to add a few chili peppers or a small bunch of herbs to a customer's purchase.

Burrito

A rolled tortilla stuffed with various ingredients.

....

Burrito means "little donkey" in Spanish. As a food, the word refers to a tortilla stuffed with ingredients such as beans, meat, cheese, onions, and peppers. Theories on how the food got its name vary. One says a Mexican street vendor in the early 1900s wrapped his food in flour tortillas to keep it warm and then put it on a donkey's back for travel. Migrant workers from Mexico helped popularize burritos in the United States.

OCTOBER 15

Cafeteria

A dining venue where customers order from a counter or serve themselves and pay before eating.

....

America's first *cafeteria* opened during the 1893 World's Columbian Exposition in Chicago. Entrepreneur John Kruger created a self-service dining area, which he called a cafeteria (a Mexican Spanish word for "coffee store"). Eating in cafeterias became trendy in the early 1900s after a Los Angeles restaurant gave customers trays to carry food chosen from a long counter. In France, cafeterias called *canteens* became popular in schools that offered food to children in need. Fast food and take-out restaurants led to the decline in cafeterias between 1960 and 1980, but cafeterias remain common at colleges, hospitals, museums, and other institutions.

Rosemary

A fragrant evergreen native to the Mediterranean, whose leaves, twigs, and flowers are used for cooking, medicine, and herbal preparations.

Salvia rosmarinus, the botanical name for *rosemary*, comes from two Latin words meaning "sea" and "dew," likely because this shrub grows well near the Mediterranean Sea. Its scent has been described as woodsy, with hints of pine, pepper, mint, and other herbs.

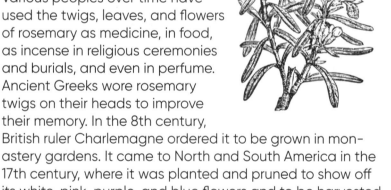

Various peoples over time have used the twigs, leaves, and flowers of rosemary as medicine, in food, as incense in religious ceremonies and burials, and even in perfume. Ancient Greeks wore rosemary twigs on their heads to improve their memory. In the 8th century, British ruler Charlemagne ordered it to be grown in monastery gardens. It came to North and South America in the 17th century, where it was planted and pruned to show off its white, pink, purple, and blue flowers and to be harvested for use in kitchens and herbal preparations.

Today, some herbalists recommend wearing a bag of rosemary while studying for a test or to keep negative energy away. Meanwhile, chefs use the herb in soups, stews, and lamb and chicken dishes, as well as alcoholic beverages.

OCTOBER 17

Pandemonium

A loud uproar or tumultuous situation; hell.

....

Pandemonium comes from the Greek word *pan* meaning "all" and the Latin word *daemonium* meaning "evil spirit." The word first made its appearance in 1667 as a literary coinage in "Paradise Lost," by English poet John Milton. *Pandaemonium* was introduced as a palace in Hell where demons lived. Over time, the word has taken on a broader meaning. The reactions to a stock market crash, a surprising courtroom verdict, or a last-second sports score may be described as pandemonium, for example.

OCTOBER 18

Fatuous

Stupid, silly, absurd.

....

The word *fatuous* hasn't changed meaning very much since it was first used in the 1530s. It comes from the Latin word *fatuus*, meaning "foolish, silly." Though it looks similar, it has no connection to *fat*. In a recent news story, complaints that Apple's release of new products betrayed owners of earlier products were called "fatuous" by the company. We may describe all manner of things fatuous, including remarks, love, decisions, actions, or claims. The word was highly popular in the 1950s but became less frequently used in the late 20th century.

Cynic

A skeptic or faultfinding critic.

....

The word *cynic* has its roots in ancient Greek philosophy. Philosopher Antisthenes organized a group of like-minded people he called the Cynics. A contemporary of Plato, Antisthenes taught at a gymnasium (a kind of all-purpose school) near Athens called *Kynosarge* ("place of the dog"). The word's association with "dog" or "dog-like" eventually reinforced the popular opinion that cynics lived a coarse, dog-like lifestyle. What the Cynics actually believed was that happiness required avoiding much of typical society's greed for wealth, power, and fame. They often lived freely without any possessions. A prominent Cynic, Diogenes, took the philosophy to extremes. Considered a man of no shame, Diogenes was said to have lived in a large ceramic jar on the streets of Athens and urinated in public.

The word came into the English language in the 1500s and its meaning changed over time. As it is used today, cynic doesn't refer to someone who is shameless or living an ascetic life. It now refers to those who focus on negative outcomes or think humans act from purely selfish motives.

Fanatic

Someone showing excessive zeal or enthusiasm for something.

The word *fanatic* is used both negatively and positively today, and the etymology of the word fits. The Latin word, *fanaticus* and the French word *fanatique*, meant "from a temple" or "inspired by god." Persons of piety were called fanatics. During the 17th century, the word described someone who was possessed by a demon. In the 19th century, the English began using the word *fan* (a shortened form of fanatic) to describe sports enthusiasts.

Today the word is popular and used in many contexts. For example, an online store selling all things sports-related is called Fanatics.com, and there's a sports radio show in Philadelphia called Fanatic. Newspaper articles use phrases such as "exercise fanatic," and "fanatic film buff" as well as derogatory ones including "religious fanatics." Religious leaders in the 20th and 21st centuries from Christians to Muslims have been labeled fanatics when they take their beliefs to extremes. Leaders of cults are also called fanatics. Those who stormed the U. S. Capitol on Jan. 6, 2021, also have been called fanatics.

OCTOBER 21

Pinguid

Fat, greasy, oily.

The word *pinguid* comes from the 1600s Latin word *pinguis* meaning "fat and juicy." It was a commonly used word in the 1700s, but its subsequent popularity has waned. It still makes appearances in literary works and newspapers. The *Chicago Sun Times* recently referred to an entertainer as "pinguid." It was one of Twitter's words of the day in 2017. The occasional food writer might reference something like fish and chips as being pinguid (and therefore, quite tasty).

OCTOBER 22

Quagmire

A swampy area where one can sink; a complex or difficult situation.

The Old English word *quag* meant "a marshy or boggy spot." An old Scandinavian word, *myr* meant "bog or swamp." Today *quagmire* refers to mucky bogs and other places where people can sink into the ground. But it, probably more frequently, it also is used figuratively to describe difficult situations that are hard to escape from. The term "quagmire theory" was used by some writers to describe the United States' difficult and complex involvement in Southeast Asia during the Vietnam War.

Gambit

A strategic opening chess movement; a ploy or strategy to get the best of a rival; an opening remark.

....

Gambit is used in several contexts today, but originally it had a very specific meaning within the game of chess. The word comes from the Italian phrase *il gambetto*, which has the sense of "get a leg up on someone." Spanish took up the word, and it subsequently made its way into French. The French later modified the spelling to gambit, and it entered the English language in the 18th century spelled this way.

As noted in *The Encyclopedia for Chess Openings*, there are many types of chess gambit, including the king's gambit (which has been popular for three centuries), the Budapest, elephant, and even the fried liver.

The word has since become a metaphor for describing a ploy to gain some advantage in a situation, especially in politics. Many newspaper headlines contain the word gambit. Gambit also references a calculated, opening line in a conversation.

Susurrous

Characterized by a murmur or soft sounds.

To experience a *susurrous* sound, take a quiet walk by a slow-moving stream and listen to the soft sounds of the murmuring brook. It's no surprise that the Latin noun *susurrus* means a "hum" or a "whisper." As a noun, it is spelled *susurrus.* The word also describes soft music or whispering voices and is used when writing about nature. Indeed, American poet Henry Wadsworth Longfellow wrote about the "soft susurrus and sighs of the branches."

Varnish

An aromatic, liquid coating that dries into a clear sheen; a pretense or covering up.

The word *varnish* likely originated in the 12th century with a Latin word *vernix* ("odorous resin"). Varnish as a substance has been used since ancient times, for example by ancient Egyptians on mummy cases. One of the ingredients was a resin from tree sap. For centuries, violin makers have perfected varnishes made of resin to coat the instrument. People today use various varnishes for furniture. The word *unvarnished* can also mean honest and upfront. This usage may have first occurred in Shakespeare's *Othello*, in the lines, "I will a round unvarnish'd tale deliver of my whole course of love."

OCTOBER 26

Palooka

A third-rate boxer; someone who is clumsy, inept, or dull.

The first use of the word *palooka* likely came in the 1920s as a reference to an incompetent boxer. The word became popular when American cartoonist Hammond Fisher created a comic strip about a boxing champion named Joe Palooka in 1930. Palooka wasn't really a third-rate boxer. Instead Fisher introduced Joe Palooka as a man conned by a pool shark who is later defeated in a boxing championship. Over the years, Joe Palooka became a comic-book hero and an inspiration to small-town America. In the comic strip, Palooka enlists in the U.S. Army just before the bombing of Pearl Harbor. He gets wounded and earns an award for his bravery, but turns down a promotion because he was just doing his duty. The comic strip ran until the early 1980s, and is said to have influenced young men to become soldiers. Though millions of Americans thought of Joe Palooka as a humble, strong, patriotic man, the term "palooka" today still has its original negative connotation of someone being inept or clumsy. It's also used when referring to a horse that has little chance of winning a race.

OCTOBER 27

Galvanize

To stimulate something with electric current; to excite and propel into activity.

....

Galvanize comes from the surname of Italian scientist Luigi Galvani. The coinage marks his major discovery: that electricity can be produced by a chemical reaction. Galvani and his wife Lucia discovered by experimentation that muscles in the legs of dead frogs would move when electric current was applied to them. Over time, the term broadened so that it can now be used figuratively. A coach's pep talk might galvanize players, for example. The word also has a specific meaning in chemistry. Galvanized steel has been coated with a thin layer of metal, such as zinc, to keep it from rusting.

OCTOBER 28

Zaftig

Plump.

....

Now used to denote a woman who is overweight, back in the 1930s, this word of Yiddish origin was used to describe an attractive female with curves. It comes from *zaftik,* which literally means "juicy," and it evolved from *zaft—* "juice"—and Middle High German's *saft*) Such a woman might also be described as buxom, or more understatedly, well proportioned.

Feisty

Spunky, courageous, spirited, unafraid.

The word *feisty* might come from any number of obsolete words including *fice*. That particular word was defined as "a small windy escape backwards, more obvious to the nose than the ears" in an 1811 slang dictionary. Fice has also been used in the southern United States to refer to a small hunting dog. The word's creation probably owes something to both of those words. It can be traced back to around the end of the 19th century. Perhaps the spunkiness of small hunting dogs played a part as well, but no one knows for certain. None of its current meanings connote flatulence.

An American journal in 1889 referred to one of former President Benjamin Harrison's law partners as "ficety." That apparently meant spirited. Harrison later appointed his law partner to the U.S. Supreme Court. Word scholars note that feisty can have a negative or positive connotation, depending on who is being described and for what purpose.

Electric

Pertaining to energy created from charged particles; stimulating, exciting, or charged with strong emotion.

Since antiquity, humans have experienced and created *electric* phenomenon. Ancient Egyptians, for example, learned that electric fish could shock the human body, and used this knowledge to treat headaches. Ancient Greeks discovered that amber, when rubbed, could somehow attract other objects. The Greek word for amber is *electron*. This became *electrum* in Latin. This source word was the basis for the coinage that entered the English 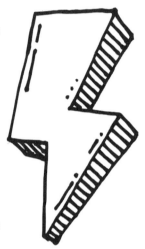 vocabulary in the 17th century. English mathematician William Gilbert used the word *electricus* in his 1600 book *Of Magnate*. He defined this word as "the property that has an object to attract others when being rubbed." In 1646, Sir Thomas Browne first used the word *electricity*.

The word enjoyed frequent and expanding usage throughout the 19th century, as the physical properties of the phenomena were explored and understood in greater depth. At some point along the way, the word acquired an emotive sense that could be used to describe a state in which things were hair-raisingly exciting, as in an electric performance by an orchestra or an electric atmosphere in the football stadium.

Casket

A small box for jewels; a water-tight vessel; a coffin.

Casket comes from the French word *casque*, meaning "helmet." The word was used in the middle of the 15th century to describe a watertight vessel holding liquids, or a small container for jewels.

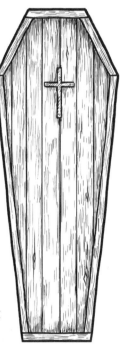

The word is now most often used interchangeably with *coffin*, which comes from a French word of the same spelling, meaning "basket." The English began using the word coffin to define a box that displays and is used to bury a corpse. Coffins have been around since ancient Egypt when bodies were wrapped and then placed in a sarcophagus (functioning essentially as a coffin). The word casket was likely introduced by an undertaker. In 1863, American novelist Nathaniel Hawthorne called a casket a "modern phrase, which compels a person to shrink from the idea of being buried at all."

Caskets and coffins are made of wood such as oak and mahogany or metal such as stainless steel. Both are lined inside with cloth upon which a body is laid. A difference between the two is that caskets typically have hinged lids, while coffins have removable lids.

Budget

Written financial plan, especially by individuals, businesses, nonprofits, and government.

....

The word *budget* went from simply meaning "small bag," to a general financial and operations catchall term. In Old French, *bougette* meant "leather pouch." A few centuries later, it took on the meaning of statement of expenses and income, referring to an English treasury minister who kept his paper budget in a leather wallet. In the 1960s, budget took on the meaning of "inexpensive." Accountants today deal with myriad budgets from fixed to flexible to rolling. Budget is also now used as a verb—people can budget their time, calorie intake, materials, or list of things to do.

NOVEMBER 2

Catachresis

A mixed metaphor; the use of a word outside of its usual context.

....

When someone takes a word or phrase outside its usual context, using it in a sense other than the intended one, he or she is employing *catachresis* (from a Greek word for "abuse"). Catachresis can be done deliberately, setting up an outlandish comparison for effect, or it may simply be a mistake. When Hamlet says, "I will speak daggers to her," the reader understands immediately that he intends to be hostile, even violent, in his speech, though daggers cannot actually be spoken. In this case, although the word is logically misused, it is figuratively effective.

Ronin

An outcast or outlaw; in feudal Japan, a wandering samurai without a master, in modern Japan, someone who fails a college entrance or is unemployed.

In Japanese, the word *ronin*, derives from roots meaning "wave man." The word was used beginning in 1185 to describe a Japanese laborer who deserts his master. Ronins were considered beneath samurais, who belonged to a prestigious military class. In time, however, a samurai who lost his master due to dishonor or death also came to be called a ronin. The samurai either found another master, became a bodyguard, or entered a life of crime. In the 18th century, 47 ronins avenged the death of their master, who was ordered by a powerful court official to kill himself. The ronins killed the court official, and then were ordered to kill themselves. The story became a symbol of loyalty and sacrifice. A festival on Dec. 14 commemorates the event. Although the samurai class was abolished in the 19th century, the word is still used in Japan today to describe students who failed college entrance exams, people who lost jobs or would-be lawyers who failed the bar exam.

NOVEMBER 4

Dandelion

A plant in the genus *Taraxacum*; usually used to refer to *Taraxacum officinale*, the common dandelion.

The name of this plant, generally perceived as a weed, comes from the French *dent de lion,* meaning "lion's tooth." The English spelled the phrase with a *d,* making it *dend de lion* and eventually shortening it to *dandelion.* Surprisingly, however, the name doesn't apply to the well-known yellow flower of the most commonplaces species of the plant, but to the saw-toothed leaf attached to the plant.

NOVEMBER 5

Hallelujah

An interjection of praise.

Hallelujah is originally a Hebrew phrase, from the root word *halal,* meaning "praise" or "boast." The short form of God's name, Jah, is added, so the precise translation is "Let us praise the Lord." In the Hebrew scriptures, it appears more than twenty times in Psalms 104–150, usually at the beginning or end of a psalm. This makes scholars think it was already a ritual phrase, calling people to worship. Its only New Testament use is in Revelation 19:1–6 (written as Alleluia in many translations), where God's ultimate victory over evil is celebrated.

Enthusiasm

Strong, fervent excitement.

....

As with so many other words, the meaning of the word *en-thusiasm* has gradually changed over time, going up and down in intensity. It may be diluted these days, but historically it had a specific and strong meaning.

Borrowed from the Greek *enthusiasmos,* the word first appeared in English texts in 1579 and meant, more or less literally, "possession by a God." The word was soon anglicized but maintained this divine denotation, as the following 1620 use demonstrates: "The Bacchanals runne thorow the streets raging and storming, full of the Enthusiasme of their god."

By the early 1700s, the use of enthusiasm was no longer limited to instances of religious ecstasy, but it still carried with it plenty of force, referring to "rapturous intensity of feeling in favour of a person, principle, cause, etc.; passionate eagerness in any pursuit, proceeding from an intense conviction of the worthiness of the object." Although the *Oxford English Dictionary* stipulates this as the "principle current sense," such a definition seems excessive when it is applied to a beer enthusiast or sports car enthusiast, or any of the other enthusiasts out there today. Or maybe, just maybe, we're simply underestimating these enthusiasts' enthusiasm.

Magazine

A periodical journal.

The original meaning (from the Arabic *makhzan,* or "storehouse") was altered by 1583 to that of a "place where goods, particularly military ammunition and supplies, are stored." In fact, the word is still used to denote a metal receptacle for bullets inserted into certain types of automatic weapons. The most common current definition of *magazine* dates back to the publication of the very first example of such a printed work, 1731's *Gentleman's Magazine.* The name was probably derived from the publication's being a "storehouse" of information.

Waif

A very thin person; a young homeless person.

In 1991, Kate Moss and other super-slim young models (who, in turn, had been preceded by the aptly nicknamed '60s model Twiggy) were dubbed *waifs,* a term that dates all the way back to 1376. In its original meaning, the term denoted unclaimed property, flotsam, or even a stray animal or person. By 1784, it referred to someone, particularly a child, who had no home or community. Since children who have no one to look after them are naturally thin, the word came to refer to the physique of such people.

Pabulum

Nutrients for plants and animals; something that sparks the intellect; something bland or weak, especially in politics.

....

Pabulum comes from the Latin word *pablum,* a word that originally meant food or fodder. Its first use in English was in the 17th century and referred to nourishment for plants and animals. A few decades later, writers used the word figuratively to describe what we've come to know as "food for thought" or mental pabulum. In a semantic turnaround, the word also took on the meaning of being bland. That happened when a new baby cereal called Pablum was created and marketed in the 1930s. The food was nutritious, but it was also considered bland.

The spellings pablum and pabulum have both been used with the same general meaning, but pablum seems to show up more frequently in popular culture. In 1970, vice president Spiro Agnew used the word in a speech referring to a report about the unrest during the Nixon era. "It is sure to be taken as more pablum for permissiveness," Agnew is quoted as saying.

NOVEMBER 10

Kiosk

Small public structure offering information and items for sale, often with interactive computer screens.

⋯⋯⋯⋯⋯⋯⋯⋯⋯⋯⋯⋯⋯⋯⋯⋯⋯⋯⋯⋯⋯⋯⋯⋯⋯⋯⋯⋯⋯⋯⋯⋯⋯⋯

The French word *kiosque*, (subsequently changed to *kiosk* in English), likely came from the Turkish word *koshk*, meaning "pavilion or summer home." The first kiosks, including those built in Egypt thousands of years ago, were buildings with open walls supported by pillars. Examples of early kiosk architecture can be seen worldwide. In English, the word has broadened in application to include any kind of small booth or stand that functions as a retail location, information station, or place where one might check out a library book, purchase tickets, or pay for parking.

NOVEMBER 11

Loiter

To stand or move slowly around seemingly with no purpose. In aviation, a phase of flight.

⋯⋯⋯⋯⋯⋯⋯⋯⋯⋯⋯⋯⋯⋯⋯⋯⋯⋯⋯⋯⋯⋯⋯⋯⋯⋯⋯⋯⋯⋯⋯⋯⋯⋯

The word *loiter* goes back to the early 15th century and may trace back to the Dutch word *loteren* ("loose, erratic"), though the etymology is unclear. Another derivative may be the Old English *lutian* ("lurk"). Yet another is the German adjective *lotar* ("empty or vain"). These source words have an overlapping sense, and there's no doubt that loiter often has a certain negative connotation. A *loiterer* may be doing the same thing as a *sightseer*, but while the latter is simply having fun, the former presents a shade of the undesirable.

Junk

Something unwanted, of poor quality or little value.

The word *junk* has come a long way from its original, mid-14th-century nautical meaning ("a piece of old rope or cable"). It's possible the word is related to the Old French word *junc* ("reed or something having little value"). By the late 1600s, junk also referred to garbage from boats, and by the late 1800s, the word often meant any kind of garbage, including something that is reusable. Junk, at first a noun, slowly also became an adjective. We are now inundated with junk food and junk mail, for example. Junk as a verb means "to throw away something."

Junk has a second meaning and etymology. As "a seagoing Chinese sailing ship," the word comes to us from the Portuguese *junco*, which in turn came from the Malay *jong*. The two words have an overlapping maritime focus, but are unrelated.

NOVEMBER 13

Kindergarten

A school for children ages 4-6 whose purpose is to prepare them for first grade.

German teacher Friedrich Frobel coined the word *kinder-garten,* meaning "garden of children" in 1837 to describe his method for developing intelligence in young children. Before then, children did not go to school in many countries until they were 7 years old. In 1840, Frobel opened the Child Nurture and Activity Institute in Germany and later changed the name to Kindergarten. Frobel's Kindergarten included hands-on activities such as working with clay and string to develop self-expression, creativity, social participation, and motor skills. England's first kindergarten opened in 1850. American schools began including kindergarten in 1868.

NOVEMBER 14

Lounge

To dally idly; an establishment for relaxation.

Lounge can be traced to the 1500s from the French word, *longis,* which means "an idle, stupid dreamer." It's used mostly in verb or adjective form today to describe places or actions in a recreational context. In contemporary usage, someone who lounges isn't considered an idle or stupid person, but other negative connotations do exist. For example, a *lounge lizard* (a 1917 coinage) referred to men who hung around tea rooms and other social places to seduce women. Lounge, used as a noun, refers to a place to relax, often where alcohol and live music are available.

Talisman

An object with magical or religious powers thought to bring good luck or stave off evil.

Tilsam ("charm") was an Arabic word that derived from the Greek word *telesma* ("religious rite or payment"). Altered forms of the word have appeared in French, Spanish, and German. The English spelling comes directly from the French *talisman*.

The word has gained traction in multiple languages, perhaps because the practice of using consecrated objects of spiritual significance is widespread across the world. Muslims use talismans such as necklaces or small pouched objects to obtain good health or protection from evil. A lucky rabbit's foot could be considered a talisman. Medieval doctors might have prescribed talismans to be worn during pregnancy or conception. Medieval palaces were often designed with talismans such as serpents to ward off evil. Talismans might be made of just about any natural material, like precious stones, plants, bones or teeth, or pieces of paper.

Haiku

An unrhymed poem with three lines, typically with the first and last lines containing five syllables and the middle line containing seven syllables.

Haiku is meant to express much in few words. This amazingly profound and elegant poetry form originated in Japan in the 1600s, developing as a reaction to traditional poetry forms deemed too long and elaborate. Its name is based on the Japanese word, *hokku*, meaning "first verse."

Traditional haiku typically takes a natural setting, seasons, or natural objects as its theme. A classic example of the ideal haiku is "The Old Pond," by Matsuo Basho, one of the form's greatest artists:

An old pond
a frog jumps into the pond
Splash! Silence again.

The aim of haiku is to describe a brief moment or scene with imagery that leads to enlightenment. The fact that this highly focused and elevated art form has achieved worldwide fame is surprising, if not wonderful.

Cataract

A waterfall; a medical condition in which the eye lens becomes cloudy, causing blurred vision.

The word *cataract* originates from the Latin word *cataracta* meaning "waterfall, floodgate." The Greek source word is *katarhaktes*, a word meaning much the same thing, but also meaning "portcullis." This sense emerges in the medical definition of the word; a cataract on the eye obstructs or hinders vision just as the grating of a portcullis blocks the sight of or passage into a building. It might also have arisen due to the similarity between the appearance of cloudy water and a cloudy eye lens.

NOVEMBER 18

Feculent

Containing impurities including fecal matter, worthless.

The word *feculent* comes from the Latin word *faeculentus,* meaning "abounding in dregs." Its meaning hasn't changed much. A peaty bog, vomit stain, dog patch, or an unflushed toilet can be feculent. Figuratively, criminals have been called feculent, and so has war. In 2012, a *Huffington Post* article on feculent cell phones revealed that fecal bacteria were found on one-sixth of cell phones examined. Considering the general sense of disgust associated with the word, it's no wonder some politicians have been branded "feculent."

Apologue

A story that generally features animals or inanimate objects behaving in ways that should serve as a lesson to readers.

....

The Greek word for fable or tale is *apologos,* and our word *apologue* made its way from that Greek word to the Latin to the Middle French and ultimately to English. The line that now distinguishes an apologue from a *fable* or a *parable* is indeed a fuzzy one. Roughly speaking, apologues usually feature animal characters, while parables feature human characters. Typically, they now both fall under the larger umbrella category of fable.

"The Tortoise and the Hare" is a classic example of an apologue by Aesop: A tortoise, tired of being mocked by a hare, challenges him to a race. The overly confident hare stops to take a nap and wakes to find that the tortoise is about to cross the finish line, and the hare has lost. The moral that most people remember from this story is "slow and steady wins the race." This moral has shown astonishing longevity, considering the story was probably first told more than 2,500 years ago! *Animal Farm,* published in 1945, is a lengthier (and grimmer) apologue.

Jukebox

A machine that plays music from a selection usually when a coin is inserted.

Anyone who has watched reruns of *Happy Days* knows what a jukebox is. Richie Cunningham and his friends would put a coin in a machine, choose what they wanted to hear from a list and the music would play. Word scholars aren't absolutely sure how this coinage arose. *Jukebox* may have been derived from the word *juke* ("rowdy" or "dance"). Coin-operated player pianos served as precursors to jukeboxes. Manufacturers didn't like the term, "jukebox." But it stuck and became the stuff of memories for American soldiers abroad who missed dancing to music from jukeboxes. At one time, 75 percent of records produced in America could be found in jukeboxes. The music wasn't just *Happy* Days-style rock, but also blues, classical, and jazz. As new ways to listen to music such as the portable cassette player were invented, jukeboxes took a back seat. They are still made and sold today, often as novelties or to be featured in an old-fashioned diner. Some people expect jukeboxes will disappear altogether, but considering the nostalgia appeal of vinyl, maybe not.

Lucubration

A labor-intensive study; work produced by the study; pompous or faulty writing or belief.

....

Lucubration entered the English vocabulary in the 1590s via the Latin *lucubrare* ("work by lamplight, night work"). One could say that Abraham Lincoln was an adherent of *lucubration*, meaning he read and studied by candlelight long into the night. By the 1800s, the word also meant "intense study at any time of day" as well as "writings resulting from such study." The word enjoyed regular usage in the 19th century, though the word is more obscure now.

When used today, the word often has a negative connotation and might be used to ridicule someone's work. For example, in his 2011 novel, *The Sense of Ending*, one of author Julian Barnes' characters proclaimed, "Spare us your sentimental lucubrations." We might now call someone's lucubrations superstitious, rambling, or ponderous, rather than intense, profound, or illuminating.

A LIGHT FACT

....

Within lucubration is the Proto-Indo-European root *leuk* ("light, brightness"). A few of the words this root provides include *elucidate, illuminate, illustrate lightning, lucent, lucid, lumen, luminary, lunar, luster,* and *translucent.*

Kvetch

A person who complains frequently; to complain.

....

A *kvetch* is a person who always complains, and that constant, habitual complaining is called kvetching. It comes from the Yiddish word *kvetshn,* which means "to press or squeeze," which in turn derives from a German term. The term kvetching shows up in English print sources about 1950, although the phenomenon of kvetching is timeless.

NOVEMBER 23

Lupine

Having wolf-like qualities.

....

Lupine comes from the French *lupin,* which derives from the Latin *lupus.* All of these words reference the wolf, or wolf-like characteristics. A toothy smile or ravenous appetite might be called lupine. Lupine qualities might be heard in a rock singer's voice, observed in an outlaw's behavior, or seen in an angular and narrow face.

As a noun, the word also may refer to the common garden flower (genus *Lupinus*), which got its name due to the fact that it was once thought to "wolf" the soil of its nutrients.

Turkey

A wild or domesticated poultry suitable for eating; three consecutive strikes in bowling; slang for a foolish person or a failure.

Of course the word *turkey* doesn't just come up during Thanksgiving. It's used in a variety of ways—from calling someone a turkey to naming three bowling strikes in a row a turkey. The word came into the English language in a fairly complicated way. It may have existed in English as far back as the 1300s, as a reference to the lands of or peoples known as the Turks. The name could have come from the Latin term *turcus* ("strength").

The word, as applied to the bird, was in firm use in English by the middle of the 16th century. The New World birds had arrived in England by this time, but via a complicated trading network: they came from Spain by way of North Africa (then under the control of the Ottoman Turks), and by erroneous association acquired the name of the country of the Turks. It's an unlikely derivation, but in those days, new foods and materials traveled by circuitous trade routes.

Raze

To utterly destroy something.

....

Raze came into English from Anglo-Norman, and is ultimately Latin in derivation. According to the *Oxford English Dictionary,* it is first found in written English in the late 14th century, and it comes from words meaning "to scrape," "to erase," or "to level"—the word *razor* comes from the same root. It's fairly common to come across the usage "raze to the ground." But since to raze is to completely destroy a building, or the fortifications of a village in wartime, or whatever else, the word alone suffices.

Guillotine

A machine that uses a blade to behead someone.

....

Contrary to popular belief, the French physician Dr. Joseph Ignace Guillotin did not invent, nor did he die from, this deadly device. Rather, he passionately entreated the French government to develop a more merciful manner of carrying out executions than the swords and ropes used at the time. The device was actually invented by Dr. Antoine Louise but a host of popular songs calling the new execution machine "La Guillotine" cemented the name with the public. After his death, Guillotin's family unsuccessfully tried to have the French government officially change the name of the device.

NOVEMBER 27

Ken

Knowledge, wisdom, range of sight.

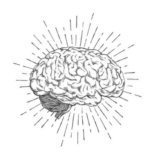

If *ken* looks similar to *know*, that's because the two words are cognate. The related German word *kennen* means "to know" and an Old English word *cennan* meant "to tell or make known." The Proto-Indo-European root *gno-* shows up in many other languages too. Some related words used in English today include *acquaint, cognition, connoisseur, could, gnome, gnostic, ignorant, narrate, noble, notice, quaint,* and *recognize.*

Today, the word is essentially a synonym for know. In the 16th century, ken primarily meant "range of sight" (especially from a boat). As a noun, the word grew in usage over the course of the 19th century. Mark Twain, for example wrote "little things, trifles, slip out of one's ken" in *The Prince and the Pauper*. Ken is often used in conjunction with beyond, as in "beyond my ken." Though usage has dwindled in this country, you might hear it in parts of Scotland, as when someone says "Ken what I mean?"

NOVEMBER 28

Jubate

Having a mane or hair resembling a mane, hairy.

The Latin word *jubatus* means "having a mane," and that's close to what the word *jubate* means in the world of zoology. Entomologists describe various insects with long, hanging hairs, as being jubate. The trait might need to be seen with a magnifying glass. The word can be found in zoological dictionaries. In other contexts, jubate means very hairy. The legendary Big Foot or Sasquatch certainly can be called jubate, and unkempt men with long hair also have been referred to as jubate.

NOVEMBER 29

Kudos

An expression of congratulations.

In his Greek epic poems, *The Iliad* and *The Odyssey*, Homer wrote, "May the gods give you glory." For the word *glory*, he used the Greek word *kydos*." The word *kudos* likely entered the English language at the end of the 18th century via academic jargon at British universities. Students who studied Homer's work began using the word to praise accomplishments. The word became popular in the United States around the 1920s and is used today to praise employees, students, and colleagues for their achievements.

Chimera

A mythical creature; something composed of incongruous parts; an animal with two sets of DNA; something impossible to achieve.

In Greek mythology, a *khimaira* was a fire-breathing creature with a goat's body, a lion's head, and a dragon's tail. Other ancient cultures, like China and Egypt, mentioned such animals. We derive the word from the French word *chimere*. From this specific Greek invention, the word has broadened in meaning to include any type of grotesque monster-like creature composed of different animal parts.

Today, the word often references something that has notably disparate parts. To take an example, a woman who needed a kidney transplant underwent routine testing and discovered that she could not be the mother of two of her three sons. This was due to her having different sets of DNA in her blood cells compared to other tissues in her body. In these extremely rare cases, the subject is called a chimera. Animals like tortoiseshell cats and some types of sponges may have this condition as well.

The word chimera is also used to mean an unrealistic wish. Wishing for permanent world peace or an unlimited supply of cheap energy might be called chimeras.

DECEMBER 1

Trice

A brief moment, immediately.

....

Trice is used today to mean "now," typically in the familiar expression "in a trice." The word likely comes from the Middle Dutch word *trisen*. This word didn't then mean immediately, but rather was used as a verb meaning "to haul up and fasten with a rope," or as a noun meaning "nautical pulley." Since the act of hauling rope was likely done briskly in a maritime setting, the tone of the action itself probably attached itself to the meaning.

DECEMBER 2

Vagrant

A poor person who is typically without a job or home; an animal outside its normal range.

....

The word *vagrant* probably comes from the French word *vagarant*, meaning "wandering around." In English, it often has a negative connotation and has been used to describe the homeless, but in a problematic sense. Rather than just being an unfortunate without a home, a vagrant is someone who is somehow socially outlying or associated with criminality—somewhere between the more neutral *transient* and the pejorative *bum*.

Chauvinism

An attitude of superiority based on a quality such as gender, region, or national origin.

....

Though we're used to hearing about male *chauvinism* these days, the term chauvinism originally stood for pig-headed nationalism. It is an eponym stemming from legendary French soldier Nicolas Chauvin, one of Napoleon's staunchest supporters.

According to the (perhaps apocryphal) Chauvin legend, there was nothing this zealous patriot wouldn't withstand for the benefit of his country and his leader. During his tenure as a soldier in the French Revolution and Napoleonic Wars, Chauvin sustained wounds on 17 separate occasions, lost fingers, and had his face disfigured, all the while maintaining his commitment to a cause that was becoming increasingly unpopular.

Upon its entrance into the English lexicon, which the *Oxford English Dictionary* dates to 1870, the word chauvinism bore a definition directly attributable to Chauvin and his legendary exploits: "Exaggerated patriotism of a bellicose sort; blind enthusiasm for national glory or military ascendancy; the French quality which finds its parallel in British 'Jingoism.'" Today, however, chauvinism has acquired a more generic sense, that of blind loyalty to one's own kind or cause. Consequently, there are now many kinds of chauvinism, including cultural chauvinism, scientific chauvinism, and national chauvinism, to name just a few.

DECEMBER 4

Engine

A machine that turns energy into force and motion.

This word was once used in reference to wit or inborn talent. In the 13th century, however, *engine* (from the Latin *ingenium*, or "the powers inborn") was used for military mechanical devices. William Shakespeare used the word to reference both meanings. It was not until the mid–18th century that "engineer" appeared in reference to those who built and operated machinery and public works, although the word was previously used to describe someone who devised intricate schemes.

DECEMBER 5

Abracadabra

A magical incantation.

The magical word of magicians is one of the few words completely without meaning. Thought to invoke the mystical powers of infinity, the word was first recorded in the second century AD by the poet Quintus Severus Sammonicus. People carved it on amulets called Abraxas stones. Theories abound—one is that the word is a corruption of the Hebrew words for Father (*Ab*), Son (*Ben*), and Holy Spirit (*Ruach Acadsch*)—but no one truly knows how this word came to be.

DECEMBER 6

Ontology

The study of existence and reality; in science, a set of definitions and relationships for terminology.

In the famous phrase "To be or not to be," Shakespeare's Hamlet was contemplating suicide. But perhaps he also was practicing *ontology*, which in a broad sense means coming to terms with the idea of being.

The word comes from Greek *onto*, which loosely translates as "being" or "that which is" and *-ology*, meaning "discourse." Philosophers have been confusing themselves about being and that which is since the early days of philosophy. Ancient Greek philosophers held a number of ideas about existence and reality. One idea posited that existence is eternal and another said that existence is called into being by thought. Plato wrote that being is a form in which all existent things participate. That was apparently helpful to know for some people.

Ontology is now a branch of philosophy that delves into the nature of reality and considers how we might learn about existence. The word has specialized usages in scientific disciplines like medicine, biology, and technology.

Awesome

Incredible, amazing, overwhelming, or remarkable.

....

Everything from movies and video games to the weather and what you ate for breakfast this morning can be, and often is, described as *awesome*. But the original meaning of awesome was more literal, as it did mean "full of awe, profoundly reverential." The *Oxford English Dictionary* has this initial meaning dating back to the late 16th century, a time when the suffix *-some* was proving productive in the formation of adjectives from nouns.

Variations emerged over the years as the word took a crooked path to its current destination. The 17th century saw an increase in awesome's versatility, as it acquired the meaning "inspiring awe; appalling, dreadful, weird." That sense, while not entirely obsolete today, is far less common than the watered-down awesome (that began appearing in the latter half of the 20th century).

It's a small step from this watered-down use to "trivial use," which is the sense we are so familiar with now. Today's awesome, an enthusiastic term of commendation, can bear as much or as little weight as the user ascribes to it. It is perhaps most commonly used as a synonym for another popular slang word that hasn't made quite such a steep journey: *cool.*

DECEMBER 8

Saccharine

Sugary; overly sweet; used both literally and metaphorically.

....

Saccharine was first recorded in the 17th century and actually means "of or like sugar." It is derived from the Latin *saccharum* (sugar), which came from the Greek *sakkharon.* It is related to the Sanskrit *sarkara,* which referred to gravel or grit in the fourth century. The artificial sweetener doesn't have an *e* at the end, but the word was first used in that form in 1885.

DECEMBER 9

Nag

To repeatedly ask or order someone to do something, in a complaining tone; one who nags.

....

The word *nag* derives from the Scandinavian *nagga,* which translates as "to gnaw." During the Middle Ages, many of the houses had thatched roofs. Rats and squirrels would sometimes burrow into these roofs, and late at night, people could hear them as they gnawed and chomped on the straw. In fact, the noise was annoying and would keep people awake. Now, the word serves as a perfect description of constantly being verbally gnawed at by another (the "nagger").

Nag is also a word for an old horse; in that usage, it derives from the Dutch *negge,* meaning a horse.

DECEMBER 10

Volunteer

To offer or agree to do unpaid work; the person who makes the offer to do unpaid work.

....

The word *volunteer* dates to the beginning of the 17th century and originally referred to soldiers who had enlisted themselves of their own free will. English borrowed the word from the French *voluntaire,* which in turn came from the Latin *voluntarius,* meaning "of one's own free will." By 1638, the word was being used broadly to refer to anyone who offered his or her service without being under obligation to do so. Samuel Johnson includes volunteer in its verb form in his 1755 *A Dictionary of the English Language* with the definition of "to go for a soldier."

DECEMBER 11

Paraprosdokian

A kind of wordplay in which a sentence starts out seeming to say one thing, but then the end of the sentence changes the meaning of what's come before.

....

This wonderful word comes from two Greek roots meaning "beyond" and "expectation"; this makes sense, because it's not a *paraprosdokian* if it's not unexpected. One classic example is comedian Will Rogers's quip, "I belong to no organized party. I am a Democrat." Another is Groucho Marx's saying, "She got her good looks from her father . . . he's a plastic surgeon."

Fake

Something that is not actually true or genuine.

The origins of *fake* are spicier than most words. It's uncertain just where the word ultimately traces back to, but it seems to have a strong association with the criminal underworld of London. The word has had so many spellings and meanings that it's hard to point to a single defining first usage, but by the 18th century the word was circulating in London as a verb. The shifty nature of thieves' slang meant that the word was used for quite a few things. Its various early meanings might include robbing, swindling, sprucing up (with intent to deceive), plundering, counterfeiting, disfiguring, wounding, shooting, or killing. These usages definitely illustrate the word's criminal origins. By the early 19th century, one vocabulary compiler, James Hardy Vaux, noted that it was "a word so variously used, that I can only illustrate it by a few examples."

While the verb provided plenty of criminal color in its first century of use, it gradually trickled into mainstream usage, where it took modern form. The word was not commonly used as an adjective until the late 19th century.

Elephant

A large land mammal with big ears and a trunk, classified as *Loxodonta Africana, Loxodonta cyclotis,* or *Elephas maximus.*

....

Although its origin is shrouded in uncertainty, it looks as though the word *elephant* comes from the ancient Greek word *elephas,* meaning "ivory." The Greek word appears with this meaning in the works of both Homer and Hesiod. Writing a few centuries later, Herodotus was the first Greek author to use the word to refer to the large, gray, ivory-tusked and long-trunked animal. As the creatures became more familiar to the Greeks—Aristotle gave a thorough (if not entirely accurate) description of the giants—their moniker became solidified.

DECEMBER 14

Flak

Literally, antiaircraft fire or guns; figuratively, intense criticism.

....

The word is a German acronym for *fliegerabwehrkanone,* or "air-defense cannon." It first appeared in English-language publications in 1938, just before the outbreak of World War II, in descriptions of German armaments. Flak's metaphorical sense arose in the early 1960s, as evidenced by this quotation from an August 1964 issue of *Newsweek*: "Congressional flak aimed at the Administration's multibillion-dollar Apollo . . . program."

Vampire

As a noun, a mythological creature who drinks blood; metaphorically, a person or entity who drains another person's time, energy, or vitality; the adjective describes animals that subsist on blood, such as vampire bats.

The word *vampire* dates back to the 1700s in English, and comes ultimately from the Serbian *vampir* via German and then French. While it was first used to describe the figure from folklore, the metaphorical use of vampire has a long history as well. The *Oxford English Dictionary* includes examples dating back to the 18th century of vampire as an epithet for an overbearing or predatory person. By the mid-19th century, one of the slang definitions of vampire was "an intolerable bore or tedious person." The word even adopted a specific use in the logistics of live theater: A trapdoor in the stage that was used to suddenly hide a character was called a vampire, presumably since the trapdoor looked (and worked) like teeth that opened to swallow an actor. We still hear the term today, as when *Rolling Stone*, in an article about Goldman Sachs's supposed predatory policies, referred to the financial behemoth as "a great vampire squid wrapped around the face of humanity."

Katydid

A mostly nocturnal grasshopper-like insect that often vocalizes with its wings to attract mates, and spends much of its time on leaves.

More than 6,400 species of the *katydid*, also called the long-horned grasshopper or bush cricket, have been identified in the world. The long-legged, mostly green insects that perch on different plants are found on every continent except in Antarctica. Most katydids make various mating sounds by vibrating their wings, but the true katydid found in the eastern United States (often high in oak trees) is the one that gave the species its name. One 18th century naturalist noted the sound was like the words "Katy did" followed by the answer "Katy didn't." J.F.D. Smyth wrote in his 1784 book *A Tour in the United States of America*, that katydids gave "a loud clamour" on warm summer nights that didn't stop until the last autumn leaf had fallen off. Other katydid species vocalize differently. The greater angle-wing katydid, for example, produces a sound like a ticking watch.

DECEMBER 17

Paradiorthosis

A false correction.

If you've ever been scolded for a grammar error, and then found out you were right in the first place, you were a victim of *paradiorthosis*. The practice of paradiorthosis is unfortunately more common than usage of the word, which has all but disappeared from most working vocabularies. William Safire used the term on December 10, 2006, in his *New York Times Magazine* "On Language" column, defining it as "a correction that is itself incorrect."

DECEMBER 18

Pangram

A short sentence that includes each letter of the alphabet.

A *pangram*, or holoalphabetic sentence, includes every letter of the alphabet at least once. The term dates to the 1780s, and is a combination of the Greek terms for "all" and "writing." The most famous one may be the typing exercise, "The quick brown fox jumps over the lazy dog," and the most challenging pangrams are the ones with the fewest letters. A few others are:

1. Quick zephyrs blow, vexing daft Jim. (29 letters)
2. Two driven jocks help fax my big quiz. (30 letters)
3. The five boxing wizards jump quickly. (31 letters)
4. Pack my box with five dozen liquor jugs. (32 letters)

Jolly

Merry, happy, full of high spirits.

Jolly may derive from the Old French word *jolif,* meaning "festive, merry, or pretty." Or it may have been a word taken from a surname. It also may have come from the Old Norse word *jol* or *yule,* referring to a winter festival. The word has seen a fairly robust growth and change in usage over the centuries—one dictionary lists 19 definitions for the word. Jolly seems to show up around Christmas too, because the festivity of the season demands it. Perhaps also, repeated references to the jollity of St. Nick and his elves and unforgettable songs like "Holly Jolly Christmas" have sunk deep roots into the collective concept of the holiday.

Beginning in the 1600s, jolly was a description for the inebriated. English usage sees the word used as an intensifying adverb meaning "very" as in "jolly good fellow" or a "jolly good time." Parents have said to their children, "You jolly well better do what I tell you."

Syllabus

An outline for a course of study.

....

A professor scanning her *syllabus* for stray typographical errors before distributing it might be interested to know that this word actually originates from a printing error. In his *Ad Atticum,* the Roman philosopher Cicero had used the Greek word *sittubas* to refer to an index. In a 15th century edition of Cicero's work, a printer mistakenly wrote *syllabos* instead. Over the years, the *o* changed to a *u,* and the word was accepted and adopted to mean not just an index, but also a list of subjects in a series of lectures.

You may wonder whether the correct plural form is *syllabi* or *syllabuses.* The answer is both! (If someone "corrects" you when you use one or the other, that is an example of *paradiorthosis* in action.)

DECEMBER 21

Malapropism

The use of an incorrect but similar sounding word.

....

Irish playwright Richard Brinsley Sheridan's first play, *The Rivals,* was first performed in 1775, establishing him as a successful playwright and introducing the character of Mrs. Malaprop. Mrs. Malaprop was prone to misspeaking, substituting words she meant to use with words that sounded similar but were very different in meaning. For instance, there's "He can tell you the perpendiculars," in which Mrs. Malaprop has confused perpendiculars with particulars. Another gem is "He is the very pineapple of politeness!" (Presumably she meant to say pinnacle.) These delightful misstatements, are now known as *malapropisms.*

Mrs. Malaprop's name was, of course, deliberately chosen to evoke her talent for choosing the wrong word. It's derived from *malapropos,* meaning "inappropriate" (from the French *mal à propos*). Baseball's Yogi Berra was a master of malapropisms who once said, "He hits from both sides of the plate. He's amphibious" (meaning ambidextrous).

HASH AND EGGCORNS

....

A related term is *eggcorn,* which occurs when someone mishears or misremembers a phrase, but the new phrase makes enough sense to seem correct. One very common eggcorn is *tow the line,* which invokes images of obeying orders by pulling a rope—which seems at least as logical as the real phrase, *toe the line.*

Desert

As a verb, to abandon; as a noun, a place with little rainfall, or, what is deserved.

The verb *desert* originally came from the Latin *deserere,* meaning "to leave, forsake," such as a soldier leaving the army. This same root also gave rise to the noun form: barren, sandy deserts seemed like forsaken places. Desert is less commonly used, but equally correct, as a noun meaning "what one is entitled to or worthy of." The word comes from the French *deserver,* "to serve well." It is often used in the plural form in the phrase, *just deserts.*

DECEMBER 23

Moot

Debatable but not provable; alternately, not worth debating.

Usually used in the phrase *moot point,* the word *moot* is a very old Germanic one meaning "a meeting place." During the Anglo-Saxon period of English history, moot was used to mean "a legislative or judicial assembly, a place where decisions are made." A moot point was a point of law or justice that was to be debated at a moot. In modern English, a *moot court* was one where hypothetical legal discussions took place, and a moot point picked up its second usage, that of a point not worth discussing.

Lousy

Bad, worthless, contemptible; alternately, teeming or swarming with, full of.

The word *lousy* comes from *louse,* and the original meaning was "infested with lice," as demonstrated in William Langland's 14th-century poem *Piers Plowman: With an hode on his hed a lousi hatte aboue.* (With a hood on his head, a lousy hat above.) But the figurative meaning we use today wasn't far behind. Geoffrey Chaucer, a contemporary of Langland's, used this figurative meaning in *The Friar's Tale: A lowsy jogelour kan deceyve thee.* (A lousy juggler can deceive you.) The second, more recent sense of lousy that plays off the metaphor of infestation rather than the insect itself arose in the United States in the mid-1800s.

DECEMBER 25

Aporia

Real or feigned self-doubt and questioning.

Like many rhetorical terms, *aporia* comes to us from the ancient Greeks. In Greek, it meant "to be at a loss," coming ultimately from a word meaning "impassable." In philosophy, aporia is an insoluble problem; in rhetoric, it is a problem that may or may not have a solution, but the writer is working it out by arguing both sides before coming to a conclusion (or not). *Hamlet*'s "To be or not to be" soliloquy is a masterful use of aporia.

Cynosure

Something or someone at the center of attention, a guide, the constellation Ursa Minor.

....

Cynosure is a word originally associated with a practice of ancient seafarers who used stars in the sky to help them navigate. In Middle French, the word cynosure referred to the constellation Ursa Minor (the Little Dipper). They derived this word from 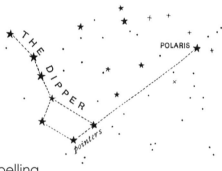 a Latin name of similar spelling, which had also been the name for the constellation. The Latin name came from a Greek formation of two words—*kyon* ("dog") and *oura* ("tail"). The constellation does indeed have a string of stars that could be visualized as a dog's tail.

The Little Dipper had been an important navigational reference for ancient Mediterranean mariners. Because of this, the word gained the sense of "prime reference point or marker." By the early 17th century, English usage of the term reflected this figurative use: a cynosure could be something or someone important or at the center of focus, just as the constellation had been to the mariners who travelled by night.

DECEMBER 27

Quiz

As a noun, a short test; as a verb, to ask questions.

The word *quiz* first appeared around the late 1700s as a noun meaning "an odd person" as well as a verb meaning "to make fun of somebody." The verb later came to mean "to look at something closely" or "to look at something mockingly"; both meanings may be related to *inquisitive,* or the Latin word *quis,* which has the sense of "Who?" This sense of asking or investigating may have led to the meaning "to ask, question." The use of quiz to mean "a set of questions that are asked, especially in school" didn't appear until the late 1800s, almost one hundred years after the word first appeared.

DECEMBER 28

Gentle

Having a mild temperament, mild, kind.

Gentle comes from the Old French *gentil,* meaning "highborn, noble," and when it entered Middle English in the 13th century, it bore this same meaning. The *Oxford English Dictionary* expounds on this original sense, explaining that gentle was "originally used synonymously with *noble,* but afterwards distinguished from it, either as a wider term, or as designating a lower degree of rank." Over time, the word broadened to refer more generally to anything kind and calm.

Shrewd

Clever; calculating.

Today, being labeled *shrewd* may or may not be a compliment, depending on the context. The adjective can be used to indicate that a person is clever and astute, or, marking a much more severe judgment of character, it can suggest that one is crafty and conniving, cold and calculating. Some 700 years ago, however, the word bore no such ambiguity. Back then, shrewd as an adjective was a categorical insult reserved for the wicked and depraved.

The word's roots are in Middle English, where it first appears around the year 1300. This adjectival form is derived from the Middle English noun *shrewe,* a word denoting a wicked or villainous person. This word is, in turn, generally understood as a figurative application of an earlier *shrewe*—ultimately from the Old English *screawa*—that denoted a small, sharp-nosed mammal. In the Middle Ages, shrews were thought to be venomous, and their bite highly injurious—hence the word's association with evil things.

Shrewd spent the next couple of hundred years undergoing slow *amelioration,* the process by which a word loses its negative meaning over time. The modern sense of shrewd—that is, "clever," or intellectually sharp—appears in the first part of the 16th century.

Nimrod

Idiot, jerk.

....

As slang, the term *nimrod* is no compliment. Yet nimrod has a considerably prouder history as an eponym. It comes from the biblical figure Nimrod, great-grandson of Noah, who is described in Genesis 10:8 as "a mighty hunter before the LORD" (KJV). According to the *Oxford English Dictionary,* this oblique reference to Nimrod lay dormant for centuries before being lexically resurrected in the 16th century. By the mid-1600s, "skilled hunter" or, more simply, "a person who likes to hunt," had emerged as the primary meaning for nimrod.

How did the word make the semantic jump from mighty hunter to mighty idiot? A widely circulated explanation attributes the shift to none other than cartoon character Bugs Bunny, who in a 1940s cartoon refers to his hapless nemesis, hunter Elmer Fudd, as a "poor little Nimrod." As the explanation goes, the audience took this use of nimrod not as a nod to Fudd's hunting hobby but as a characterization of his slow-wittedness. There is one problem here. The *Oxford English Dictionary* dates the earliest use of the dumbed-down version of nimrod to 1933 (in the play *The Great Magoo*)—about a decade before Bugs and Fudd ever crossed paths.

DECEMBER 31

Hogmanay

The Scottish celebration of New Year's Eve.

While many of us are used to lighting off fireworks to cele-brate the New Year, the Scots take *Hogmanay* to a whole other level. The etymology is obscure, probably from an Old French term referring to the last day of the year. The celebration dates back further than most modern cele-brations, including Christmas itself. Many of the traditional elements of the holiday were established when Scotland was still worshipping Pictish, Roman, and Viking gods. First Footing, for example, is an ancient tradition wherein a dark-haired stranger bearing coal at your door at mid-night is a sign that the coming year will bring you luck.

In our time, many families gather to tour one another's homes on the day, taking turns each year at the end to make a festive meal for all involved. Other people dress up like ancient sun gods for the various street festivals, while in many communities, lighting bonfires and swinging fireballs through the streets on a chain all lead up to the ringing of the bells at midnight.